GETTING STARTED
AT FLY FISHING
FOR TROUT

GETTING STARTED AT FLY FISHING FOR TROUT

Allan Sefton

ROBINSON

ROBINSON

First published in Great Britain in 2013 by Right Way,
an imprint of Constable & Robinson

This edition published in 2023 by Robinson

Copyright © Allan Sefton 2013, 2023

Illustrations © by Jim Wilde

1 3 5 7 9 10 8 6 4 2

The moral right of the author has been asserted.

A CIP catalogue record for this book
is available from the British Library.

ISBN: 978-1-47214-794-3 (paperback)
ISBN: 978-0-71602-289-3 (ebook)

Printed and bound in Great Britain by Clays Ltd, Elcograf S.p.A

MIX
Paper from
responsible sources
FSC® C104740

Papers used by Robinson are from well-managed forests
and other responsible sources

Robinson
An imprint of
Little, Brown Book Group
Carmelite House
50 Victoria Embankment
London EC4Y 0DZ

An Hachette UK Company
www.hachette.co.uk

www.littlebrown.co.uk

How To Books are published by Robinson, an imprint of Little, Brown Book
Group. We welcome proposals from authors who have first-hand experience of
their subjects. Please set out the aims of your book, its target market and its
suggested contents in an email to howto@littlebrown.co.uk

CONTENTS

FOREWORD

In my Foreword to the popular first edition of this book I said, 'What a perfect time to publish an excellent and comprehensive guide to taking up fly fishing'. It is timelier today! This second edition provides a wider breadth of advice and help for anyone thinking of taking up the sport.

The popularity of angling increased dramatically during the Covid-19 pandemic. The Environment Agency issued the highest number of rod licences for decades. The benefits of angling to both our physical and mental health were recognised by health professionals throughout the country. People who have always wanted to 'get started' did just that. Nearly 1.3 million licences were issued for England and Wales in 2021, an increase of 17 per cent on the previous year.

Many of these new anglers will have friends and family who first introduced them, but angling, especially fly fishing, is a technical sport and progress demands good coaching and regular support from more accomplished anglers.

Fortunately, our National Governing Body, the Angling Trust, provides a network of licensed coaches for all levels and well-established clubs which welcome novices. Allan Sefton is an example of an expert all-round angler who is a licensed, game fishing coach. He chairs Invicta Fly Fishing Club which has developed beginners of all ages into excellent trout anglers. Many now represent the club in friendly inter-club competitions and some have won international honours. Not surprisingly, the club, like several others adopting this approach, has enjoyed a healthy increase in its membership.

This revised, information-packed edition of Get Started at Fly Fishing for Trout starts with the basics before advancing seamlessly to more sophisticated aspects of fly fishing. The addition of the river chapters will be very welcome. There is increasing awareness of small streams and urban watercourses that hold trout. They do not only live in better known and more exclusive game rivers.

Many beginners start coarse fishing on a river or small still-water where they learn about tackle, knots, bait and how to play and return a fish. These basic skills transfer happily to fly fishing for trout. It does not matter whether you are a convert to fly fishing or an absolute beginner, this book contains all the information, guidance and encouragement needed to ignite a passion for fly fishing.

Tight lines!

David E. Moore
Life Vice-President, Angling Trust
Secretary, English Fly Fishing Association

INTRODUCTION
WHY FLY FISHING?
WHERE TO GET HELP

Mankind evolved over thousands of generations as a hunter-gatherer. We needed fish to eat. So it is no surprise that some of us are still driven to seek a relationship with our environment. It is the reason we love gardens, watch wildlife and get obsessed with catching fish.

When fishing, we're more than mere spectators. We're actively involved in a contest with a living creature. It's fascinating to try to understand why trout behave as they do and focus on what makes them vulnerable to a hunter's wiles. It tests our knowledge, skills and patience. It's a challenging pastime, enjoyed in the great outdoors, with the ultimate reward being the sense of achievement we experience when finally pulling in that elusive fish.

National Social Trends Surveys put fly fishing way up the list of sports that people would like to try. This is not surprising as fly fishing gets a good press. There are popular books, TV shows and films that extol the beauty of trout waters and the wiliness of our quarry. Fly fishing clearly provides the opportunity, now increasingly in demand, to be an active part of the countryside and not simply just another rambler admiring the view.

FLY FISHING AND WELL-BEING
A benefit of the Covid pandemic was that fishing was permitted, and many grabbed the opportunity to re-awaken their interest in fishing or take it up for the first time. The sale of fishing permits and licences rocketed. Not surprisingly, the tackle trade, fishery owners and licensed coaches all played their part in welcoming so many newcomers.

Enthusiasm was also stoked by *Gone Fishing*, a BBC 2 programme featuring Paul Whitehouse and Bob Mortimer, a love letter to the joy of angling. It was not a 'how to' guide. Instead, the series concentrated on fun, companionship and their past heart problems. Trying to catch fish, whether a triumph or a disaster, was the catalyst to their recovery and happiness.

No one has better demonstrated there is more to fishing than catching fish. Getting started takes some effort but, with some investment of time and development of skill, it transforms lives. 'Going fishing' provides an escape from woes. It creates an eternal passion to have just one more cast.

That's well-being!

SPORT FOR ALL

Angling was one of the first sports to embrace the *Sport-for-All* policy and had the required framework in place, a necessity if you want to attract government grants, before many high profile sports had left the starting blocks. Today, angling is one of the few sports where the supply of highly trained, licensed Level Two coaches exceeds the demand.

Fly fishing is certainly a sport everyone can enjoy. In the USA and Canada around 45 per cent of all fishing licences are sold to women. In the UK, although it is currently well under 10 per cent, it is rising. Fly fishing is taking off as a recovery therapy for women who have had surgery for breast cancer. The persistent reaction to their *Casting-for-Recovery* courses is how much these women have enjoyed the whole fly fishing experience and how they wish it had been part of their life before their illness.

The whole point of *Sport-for-All* is that no one should be excluded. Sport provides its greatest benefits when it is a family activity. I believe that fishing, and fly fishing in particular, provides more opportunity for inter-generational participation than any other sport. I am a grandfather who organizes days out to prove it. It costs less than taking the family to a football match!

THE ROLE OF SCHOOLS AND CLUBS

For all sports the normal way in is to join a club. Most children first play traditional sports such as soccer, rugby or hockey at school. Those with enthusiasm and talent will be encouraged to join a local club where they will get more professional coaching and entry into higher level competitions. School should also be the entry point to other sports not played in school so that permanent links become established with local clubs. Usually, this is the result of one teacher being a passionate advocate who appreciates that not everyone is suited to chasing a ball around a muddy field.

The problem for fly fishing is that most of us are not members of a club. Even if we are, the club may concentrate solely on going fishing. Providing tackle, facilities and coaching for youngsters is not on their agenda.

Nowadays, schools need to ensure that any club they link to has all the above and is safe for children. The Angling Trust's *Club Mark* status provides evidence of this. Although only few fly fishing clubs have achieved this testing standard, the numbers are growing.

Unfortunately, even clubs with *Club Mark* accreditation can struggle to build a relationship with local schools. So, if you are part of a school family, as a governor, teacher or parent, could you ask them to consider encouraging fly fishing through links with a local club as part of the extra-mural activities they offer? The Angling Trust's (www.anglingtrust.net) England Youth Flyfishing (http://englandyouthflyfishing.blogspot.co.uk/) and equivalent bodies in Scotland and Ireland can all help.

FLY FISHING IS A JOURNEY NOT A DESTINATION

Here is a surprising confession at the beginning of a book on fly fishing. When someone says, 'Take me fishing, please,' and it's for the very first time, I often take them coarse fishing for roach, perch and carp. Coarse fishers use natural baits like maggots and worms instead of artificial flies and have tackle that incorporates weights that makes getting this bait to the fish much easier than casting a fly.

I find that most coarse fishing newcomers are confidently casting and are able to use three different coarse fishing techniques in only a couple of hours. We can then move on to the serious business of catching fish.

Best of all, it will not be long before the float disappears and a brand new angler strikes into their very first fish. Quick success is important to newcomers. It is the reward for learning lessons about fish behaviour, how to present their bait and how to hook, play, land and handle a fish.

Introducing a newcomer to fly fishing is different. Until you learn to cast you cannot fly fish. And, the truth is that fly casting is not easy. Like driving a golf ball or playing football, fly casting depends on timing, smooth movement and practice. But, there is another problem too. Two elements of fly casting are counter-intuitive, which makes them hard to get right. You also need mature coordination skills which, as a rule-of-thumb, youngsters do not usually develop until they are at secondary school.

I advise strongly that younger children are taken coarse fishing. The tackle is easy for them to use, and most importantly of all, they will enjoy plenty of action and catch plenty of fish. They learn that fishing is a lifetime journey and that fly fishing is another step on the way.

This can be a tough lesson for fly fishing parents and grandparents who have no interest in coarse fishing. But, I appeal to them not to take the risk that their kids will be put off fly fishing for life by failure. If they wait I can guarantee that teenagers learn to fly cast, and to love the subtleties of fly fishing, at a pace that puts everyone else to shame.

It takes time, and hard work, for all beginners to learn to fly cast and to develop a new 'muscle memory' that will serve for a lifetime.

The good news is that, like riding a bike, once it is firmly implanted you never forget.

USE A LICENSED COACH

Because fly casting, the first hurdle to becoming a fly fisher, is a high one and the time span of the 'beginner' stage varies, even good coaches are guilty of saying, 'I'll teach you to fly fish,' when they mean, 'I'll teach you to cast.' Learning to fly fish is a rewarding, life-long process. It does not start until you can cast pretty well.

If casting is difficult, why do so few fly fishers have lessons?

A golfing novice's first port-of-call, before venturing onto the course, is the golf pro's shop to book a course of lessons which will include wise advice on a first set of clubs to fit their physique and developing skills.

The vast majority of UK fly fishers have never had a lesson in their lives. It shows and it matters!

Poor casters who cannot cope with high winds or bankside obstructions limit their choices and opportunities. More seriously, we all get older and an over-energetic, ineffective casting action can become a painful curse when rheumatism kicks in.

So if you are a fly fishing newcomer it really helps to have a few lessons with a licensed coach. The Game Angling Instructors' Association (www.gameanglinginstructors.co.uk) provides all the help you need. Coaches will also give wise advice on buying tackle. Many clubs provide free coaching. Many waters organize beginners' courses. Use them!

MANAGING EXPECTATIONS AND WHERE TO FISH

It is equally important to manage expectations. I beg newcomers to be pragmatic and try to help them set realistic targets. The best place to start fly fishing is on a small, heavily stocked fishery. Most beginners avoid the big reservoirs which demand long casting, experience and up-to-the-minute intelligence. They can be the next step in the journey.

In every county in the UK there are waters of a manageable size run by members of the Stillwater Trout Fisheries' Association (www.stillwatertroutfish.org). They welcome novices.

FISHING LICENCES

To fish legally in England and Wales two requirements need to be satisfied. Firstly, you need permission from the riparian owner or tenant of the fishing rights. This is usually in the form of a day ticket or similar permit. Secondly, you need an Environment Agency fishing licence. There are different licences (and prices) depending upon the species you wish to fish for and the duration of the licence to accommodate visiting anglers. Most trout fishers opt for an annual trout fishing licence. The Environment Agency prefers you to buy them online (www.gov.uk/fishing-licences) and to pay by direct debit so that they can keep in touch with you and provide you with information. The Agency funds fishery development, pollution control and water management from their licence income.

There are different administrative arrangements in Scotland and no national rod licence is needed. You still need permission from the owner of the fishing rights to fish for trout.

For licences for fishing in Northern Ireland, consult the Department of Culture, Arts and Leisure website (www.dcalni.gov.uk). In general, a licence is not required to fish for trout in the Republic of Ireland, except in the Loughs Agency waters in counties Donegal and Louth.

WILD CREATURES

Trout are wild creatures. They respond to weather, food availability and to physical conditions. They don't adapt their behaviour to fit your convenience. Trout fishing is easiest in the spring and autumn when insects are hatching, not during the hot days of mid-summer holidays when many small fisheries can reach an almost lethal temperature for trout when they switch off completely. Nobody can catch them. This is why many small, *and honest,* trout fisheries close down in July and August. It is why wise trout anglers carry a thermometer.

A LONG JOURNEY?
Although beginners usually develop their skills where fishing is easiest, most soon get the 'fly fishing is a journey' idea and seek out new challenges. Rivers, big lakes, wilderness waters and even the tropical, coral flats are waiting. It may become a long, joyful voyage of discovery. Make sure you enjoy every moment.

PART ONE
AT THE OUTSET

Part One aims to provide all the help needed by someone getting started at fly fishing. The first chapter describes the essential tackle and equipment and how much it costs. Chapter 2 gives details of the knots that new fly fishers must be able to tie for themselves before venturing out. It also provides hints and tips to avoid some frustrating, early problems and pitfalls.

Both chapters explain the technical terms that fly fishers use which seem like a foreign language to newcomers at first. These specialist words and phrases are highlighted and defined. More detail on some is given in the Glossary at the end of the book.

1
WHAT EQUIPMENT
DO I NEED TO BUY?

Fifty years ago fly rods were made of the finest bamboo imported from China. Craftsmen cleverly shaped long strips of tapered bamboo into a triangular cross-section so that they could be glued and bound together to make a 'built-cane' rod. The aim was a strong, straight rod which was as light as possible. The quality of the bamboo, and the taper produced by a skilled rod-builder, gave the rod tensile strength. It formed a parabolic curve when the tip was bent over and sprang back strongly when released.

The tapered fly lines available then were made of braided silk. Three sizes were made. Silk lines needed careful management. If you wanted it to float it had to be greased. It still became waterlogged after a time and fishing had to stop to dry it out and to re-grease it. Silk lines rotted if they were left wet on a reel at the end of the day. They had to be wound onto a line-dryer and stored in a dry, warm room.

Despite the craftsmanship involved, this combination was not easy to cast. The rod weighed heavily in the hand. Timing had to reflect the slow action of the flexing rod. It bent from tip to butt as the cast was made and needed time to recover as the force of the moving rod tip was transferred to the unfurling line.

Today, most rods still come from the Far East where they are mass-produced in factories by wrapping carbon-fibre cloth, a true space-age material, around tapered steel mandrels and baking it hard using epoxy resins. The resulting thin-walled tubes are astonishingly strong and light. Their carefully designed taper means a perfect marriage to a pre-determined line weight. A finished rod weighs less than 4 ounces.

A modern fly line is made by moulding a flexible, slippery plastic around a braided nylon core. They are made in fourteen sizes, each giving assurance that the casting weight of the extended line accords with a worldwide agreement. There are many variations in the shape, or profile, to serve different casting styles and modern rod designs. Most manufacturers produce floating lines and ten different sinkers. Sinking lines range from a floating line with a sinking tip to one that heads for the bottom at the rate of 7 inches per second. They need no regular treatment, are pretty tough and last for years.

Fifty years ago craftsman-built fly rods and lines were expensive, and fly fishing was an elite sport. Today you can still pay £600 plus for a perfectly finished rod that is one quarter of an ounce lighter than one you can buy for a tenth of that price. Both are effective tools. Both will last a lifetime. In fact, it is possible to buy all the essential fly fishing tackle a beginner needs for around £150.

Fly fishing is now a Sport-for-All.

BEGINNERS' TACKLE – THE ESSENTIALS
RODS

Many beginners are attracted to fly fishing by the skill and elegance of casting a *fly*. The *fly rod* and *fly line* are simple tools. They are designed to place a fly in front of a wary trout without scaring it. You need to understand how this tackle works to get started. After that, practice and experience are all that are required!

Most fly fishers buy lots of rods during their lives. The first is the most important. Buy the wrong rod and it will be difficult to learn how to cast. Bad habits develop that may never be cured. You could even give up in frustration.

Fly rods are still universally labelled and measured in imperial units. Most other measurements in this book are metric.

The fly rod has to be matched to its owner. A long, heavy rod such as our forefathers used may be fine for a big strong man but it would defeat a lesser being.

Why?

A fly rod and a thick, tapered fly line provide the force to propel a weightless fly over the water. The critical element in every cast is a flexing rod tip that 'accelerates to a stop'. The 'stop' transfers this power into the unfurling line. Achieving optimum force depends on maximizing the tensile strength of the flexing rod. The fly rod is an extension of your forearm. It acts like a lever with your elbow as its fulcrum. As the rod 'accelerates to a stop' the wrist must be stiff. If it is not, it is like trying to cast with a broken rod.

Keeping your wrist stiff at this critical moment depends upon some forearm strength. Obviously, this develops with practice but fly fishing is not a sport where bigger and stronger is inevitably better. Skill is required and this will only develop if casting is not a constant test of strength. Beginners need a rod and fly line combination that is light enough to handle easily. The length of the rod is more important than its *rating*. This makes sense. A rod is an extension of the forearm and lengthening the rod from, say, 9 feet to 10 feet makes a big difference to the forearm strength required to continually stiffen the wrist at the critical point in every cast during a day's fishing.

Fly rods are internationally *rated*, and always labelled, say as *#7 weight*. This means that the maker believes the rod should be matched with a *#7 weight* fly line labelled to the international *American Fishing Tackle Manufacturers (AFTM)* standard.

Beginners should consider both the lightest rods, rated *#1 to #3 weight*, and the heaviest, which are rated *#8 weight* and above, as specialist tools and not for them.

Almost everyone should start with a *#6 weight* 9 foot rod. Youngsters or women who are slightly built might even find an 8 foot 6 inch *#5 weight* rod easier, even though they will probably want to advance to the slightly heavier combination later. A large man would have no problems using a 9 foot *#7 weight* rod. No one should attempt to learn with a rod more than 9 feet long.

Fig. 1. A fly rod butt showing length and line 'rating'.

It is not only length and weight that are important. Your first fly rod should have an all-through *middle-to-tip action*, i.e. it should flex progressively from its tip to its middle so that you are able to 'feel' it bending as the acceleration of the rod tip and fly line build up the force of a cast. Later, you might advance to a stiffer, *tip action* rod which will provide more force for long casts but *only in response to good technique.*

Fortunately, the cheaper ranges of rods from reputable fishing tackle firms usually have a middle-to-tip action. This is the price range where the beginner should start. An excellent, top quality beginner's 9 foot #6 *weight* fly rod will cost only £80 or so. Last year's model may be 'on offer' and even cheaper!

Experience suggests that fly casting is difficult for most under-11-year-olds simply because the muscles in their forearms and their coordination skills have not fully developed. It is wise to wait until they are older rather than to force them to learn and to fail.

FLY LINES

Manufacturers rate their rods for, say, #6 weight fly lines based on the acceleration of the line in the air achieved by expert casters. Novices cannot achieve the same *smooth* rate of increase in the speed of their rod tip and they should increase the weight of line to compensate. You should match your new rod with a line which is at least one size up. Use a #7 weight line with a #6 weight rated rod and casting will be much easier initially. By the time this line wears out you may be such an expert caster that you will decide to revert to the 'correct' rating!

You should choose a *Floating Weight Forward* line. *Weight Forward* (WF) simply means that its first 10 metres or *head* tapers towards its tip. The 'weight' of this head determines its rating. The rest of its full 30 metres is a much narrower *shooting* or *running* line that enables it to fly out easily. Most fly lines used today are 'Weight Forward'. On its box a weight forward #6 weight, floating, fly line will have the shorthand label, '*WF#6F*'.

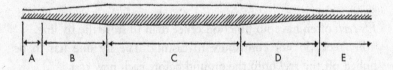

Fig. 2. The profile of a weight forward fly line.
A: Tip – 0.5 metres. B: Front taper – 1.5 metres. C: Line belly – 5 metres.
D: Rear taper – 3 metres. E: Running line – 17 metres.

Double Taper (DT) lines are also available. They have a taper at each end and a thick belly in between. They are chosen by those fly fishers who never need to cast a long way, such as chalk stream dry fly fishers. These fly lines can be reversed when the taper at one end becomes worn out.

Small water fly fishers will sometimes find a *Slow Sinking* line, labelled *Intermediate (I)*, useful (see later advice in Chapters 7 to 16 on tactics). An extra line like this should be stored on a spare spool for the fly reel chosen. There is no need to buy two complete reels.

It is false economy to buy the cheapest fly line. Good quality lines specially designed for beginners are not expensive at around £30. Best quality lines do cost more at £50 or so. They last longer and have a smoother surface which reduces surface tension and helps to achieve longer casts.

The most useful fly lines for beginners change colour at the point where the 30 foot head (approximately three rod lengths) tapers back to the finer 'shooting' line. This indicator helps the novice to cast the same length of line beyond the rod tip each time. Doing this helps achieve consistent timing, distance and 'muscle-memory'. The alternative is to mark a light-coloured line at this point using a waterproof felt-tip pen.

REELS

Fly reels often have no function other than to store the fly line.

Fly reels do not contribute to casting. The fly line has to be pulled off the reel onto the ground before each new cast.

Trout are usually hooked when some line has already been retrieved and there is loose line at your feet. Many fly fishers *play the fish by hand* or *hand line it in*. They use their free hand to keep the line tight, or to release it if necessary and, eventually, to pull the fish in. Their reel is not used at all. On occasion, when big fish are being targeted on heavy tackle, or when a very big fish is hooked and all the loose line disappears through the rod rings, it will be *played on the reel* and the reel will be used to play the fish and wind it in.

Fly reels are *centre-pin reels*, i.e. one turn of the reel means one revolution of the 'spool'. A few models are fitted with gears that speed up the revolutions of the spool.

Although fly reels do not do much for most of the time, unless you are expecting to tangle with big, fast fish, they come in a multitude of designs, quality and prices. While it is worth paying serious money for a reel equipped with a high quality, adjustable drag for a specialist approach to giant fish, it is quite unnecessary for the trout fishing beginner. Excellent beginners' fly reels are available from most reputable fishing tackle manufacturers for around £40.

Fly reels come in different sizes to accommodate the different profiles and thicknesses of fly lines. *Small* reels are for #3 to #5 weight lines. *Medium* take #6 to #8 weight and *Large* are for #9 weight and above. All reel makers supply spare spools so that you can buy several inter-changeable spools for different fly lines. Spare spools for a £40 reel will cost around £18. Today, most reels have *wide arbour spools*. This means the centres of the spools are built up. This reduces the tendency for the line to form tight memory coils when it is not on the spool.

Backing line has to be put on the reel spool before the fly line because the fly line is only 30 metres long and more line may be needed if a big, hooked fish runs a long way when being played. Most backing lines are made from cheap braided nylon. A 100-metre spool costs only £8. Fifty metres of backing line is enough on a trout reel.

LEADERS

The business end of fly fishing tackle consists of a *leader, tippet* and *fly*.

The leader is the length of transparent, thin line attached to the tip of the fly line with the artificial fly at the other. A leader is needed because the relatively thick tip of the fly line is highly visible. The fly will only be taken by a trout if the leader is invisible. The length of a leader is important. If it is long, the separation between the highly visible tip of the fly line and the disturbance it causes on landing is an advantage. But, a fine leader does not *turn over* like a thick fly line when it is cast and can fall in a heap, especially if there is a wind in your face. Choosing the right length is a balancing act.

Beginners should use a 3-metre (or 9-foot) *tapered nylon or co-polymer leader*. Its thick end is attached to the tip of the fly line. The effect is to extend the taper of the fly line into the leader itself and this is a definite advantage for a novice caster. A leader that tapers down to a *Breaking Strain (BS)* of 8 lb is about right. It costs around £2. To this you should attach a 1-metre tippet of 6 lb BS fluorocarbon line to which the fly will be tied.

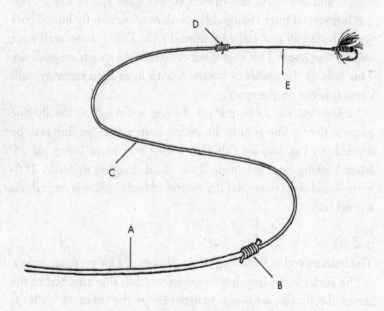

Fig. 3. Leader and tippet.
A: Fly line. B: Nail knot. C: Tapered 3 metre leader. D: Blood knot. E: Tippet.

There are two reasons for adding a fluorocarbon tippet to the end of the leader. Firstly, if the fly were tied directly to the end of the tapered leader it would get shorter every time the fly was changed, its fine tip would disappear and it would have to be replaced. Secondly, and more importantly, modern fluorocarbon line is wonderfully fine and invisible to fish. It is transparent and its specific gravity is close to that of water. A 100-metre spool of 6 lb BS fluorocarbon, which has a diameter of only 0.205 mm, costs around £18. This is not cheap, but no one denies its advantages. A hundred metres makes a lot of tippets!

FLIES

There are many, many thousands of *patterns* of *artificial flies*. Fly fishers often refer to them simply as *artificials* or *flies*. Every day brand new patterns of flies are *tied*. The recipe for each fly is known as its *dressing* and people who tie flies are therefore known as *fly-dressers*. There is an accepted formula for describing different

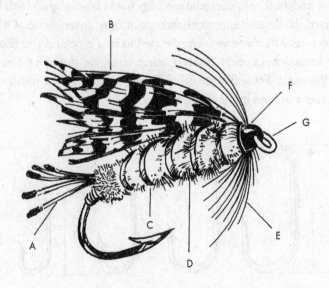

Fig. 4. A fly.
A: Tail. B: Wing. C: Rib. D: Body. E: Hackle. F: Head. G: Hook eye.

dressings which identifies it and is the recipe by which others can copy it. As most flies, and especially the earliest ones, were tied to imitate insects it is not surprising that the 'ingredients' of a fly dressing, after the hook pattern/size and the brand/colour of the tying thread, are *Tail*, *Rib*, *Body*, *Wing* and *Hackle*. Sometimes *Cheeks*, *Eyes* and *Wing Cases* are added. These labels are now universally used for all fly patterns, whether or not they imitate insects. Most imitative trout flies are tied on size 10, 12 and 14 hooks. The shank of a size 12 hook is about 8 mm long.

Hooks are sized on an even number scale. Size 2 are big sea fishing hooks and those from size 20 upwards are nearly microscopic. Occasionally trout fishers use tiny flies tied on size 16 or size 18 hooks. Many trout *lures* and other 'attractor' flies are tied on large size 8 hooks but the majority of trout flies are in the size 10–14 range. Most hooks have straight shanks but some speciality hooks labelled *grub hooks* have curved shanks to help imitate shrimps or other invertebrates. Others, known as *Klinkhammer hooks*, are used to tie a type of *dry* or floating fly that imitates a newly 'hatched' insect 'emerging' through the surface of the water. These flies are called *Emergers*. There will be much more on flies and lures in the chapters on tactics.

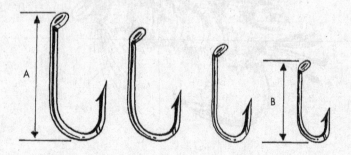

Fig. 5. Trout hook sizes.
From left to right: size 10 (A=15mm); size 12; size 14; size 16 (B=10mm).

Fifty years ago, all fly patterns were tied using 'natural' materials such as cock or hen hackle feathers, wing feathers, hair and fur often secured with some tinsel or wire. All these patterns are still used by fly fishers and they still catch trout. They are often described as *traditional* patterns. Many imitated particular species of insects.

Today, many modern fly patterns are tied using new, synthetic materials which can provide fluorescence, mobility and garish colours that were unavailable years ago even if you had access to the feathers of the most exotic birds.

Many of these 'new' flies make no pretence of imitating any living thing. They are therefore labelled as *lures* to differentiate them from *imitative* flies.

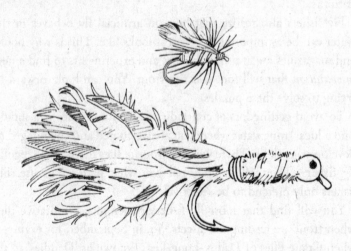

Fig. 6. A small imitative fly (hook size 16) and a lure (hook size 8).

With many thousands of patterns of flies to choose from how does the beginner select the right fly? The answer to this question is not as difficult as you think.

Every fly pattern ever tied has probably caught a trout so nothing is hopeless. Trout are a predatory, opportunist and inquisitive fish. If they are feeding aggressively almost anything that moves, or is unusual, may be grabbed. This is why newly stocked trout are found with all manner of stomach contents from plant seeds to cigarette butts. They are not hard to catch!

The other side of this coin is that such reckless behaviour is usually short-lived. All trout, even those that are feeding hard, can become infuriatingly *selective* and will ignore most artificial flies. Difficult, selective fish are what makes fly fishing for trout the challenging game it is. Difficult trout are the reason that thousands of fly dressers are constantly inventing new patterns.

Fly fishers also realize that how an artificial fly behaves in the water can be as important as what it looks like. This is why books and magazines are awash with ideas and experiments to find a new *presentation* that will fool selective trout. You can look forward to trying to solve these puzzles.

To avoid getting lots of contradictory advice on flies you should find a local trout water where you are welcomed and encouraged to develop your skills. There will be favourite flies used by the regular fly fishers. They will happily tell you what patterns to use. Fly fishers only pretend to be secretive!

You will find that most fly fishers prefer to use imitative flies when trout are feeding on insects. So, in September, for example, when Crane Flies or Daddy-Long-Legs (known as 'Daddies' to fly fishers) are being blown onto the water from nearby fields an imitation of this adult fly may be a favourite.

Similarly, colourful damselflies emerge from every pond and lake in the summer and an olive-green imitation of a damselfly larva or *nymph* may be favoured. Trout feed greedily on them when they swim up from the lake bottom to emerge as an adult fly.

In spring, *Chironomid* 'non-biting midges' or *buzzers* (named by fly fishers after the noise from clouds of flying adults) emerge in millions from every pond and lake in the UK. The larvae have spent the winter in the mud of the lake bottom. As the water warms, their pupae leave their protective tubes. They float to the surface where their skin splits to free a flying adult. Buzzer imitations in various colours are found in every trout fisher's fly box. Chapter 14 explains how to use them.

On the days when there is little insect activity, a lure may be the first choice of fly. All waters seem to have a favourite lure. Do not let this stop you experimenting with others. Chapter 13 gives advice on fishing with lures.

There are also some patterns of fly that, although tied to copy the size and shape of common freshwater insects, do not pretend to be a copy of any specific insect. These *standard* patterns are successful almost everywhere. A good example is the Hare's Ear Nymph. Guess what fur is used to dress it! Chapter 12 describes the three best nymphs in the world.

So, you should arm yourself with a dozen or so popular flies for your chosen water to get started. It will only be a start. If you follow other fly fishers, you will soon own hundreds. On average, £1 buys an artificial fly in a shop despite the fact that the hook and materials from which it is dressed cost only a few pennies. It takes nimble, skilled fingers to tie a fly. These have to be paid for!

This is why many thousands of fly fishers tie their own flies. It is a 'no-brainer' on price and, even more importantly, may be the one way to get an artificial fly that looks exactly how you want it to.

To get you started many firms sell fly collections mounted on cards. They provide proven patterns and the scope to experiment. For example, one company supplies several collections of ten flies, including buzzers, 'Daddies' and damselfly nymphs. They cost around £10 each.

There is much more on fly choice tactics in later chapters.

In summary, you are equipped to go fly fishing when you have bought a rod, reel, fly line, leaders and a few flies. You can buy the lot for around £170. Some tackle dealers sell 'beginners kits' at discounted prices in the hope you will become a permanent customer. One company offers a 20 per cent discount if you buy a rod, reel and fly line together so their excellent kit costs around £150. This comes in a presentation box and includes a rod and a reel which has already been loaded with backing and a fly line with a leader attached. A perfect gift.

OTHER KIT

One of the challenges fly fishers face throughout their lives is to stop themselves buying too much kit. As in many sports, there is always a new 'must-have' item on the market to tempt you. Most fly fishers have several rods. All, inevitably, were a vital addition to their armoury when they bought them. Mostly, they lie unused today.

Still water fly fishers, in particular, buy many different lines so that they can fish at all depths. And, every fly fisher on the planet buys a few more flies on every visit to a fishing tackle shop or favourite website. They hope that the new fly pattern they have not used before will succeed where thousands of others have failed.

To get started, rod, reel, lines and flies are the essential items. There are other wonderfully useful products and 'gizmos' that most fly fishers carry. A choice selection of them is listed in the next chapter.

Everything you need can be carried in your pockets if you buy a *fly fisher's waistcoat*. Today, almost every fly fisher has one of these great inventions. A good one costs around £70. There is a huge range of patterns and prices and some even incorporate an automatic life-jacket.

You may need a fishing bag too, even if only to carry your sandwiches and flask. However, do think about this. Wandering around with all your gear in your pockets, unencumbered by a heavy bag, is one of the joys of fly fishing. You can always go back to your car for lunch. An everyday fishing bag costs about £25, if you must.

Out of respect for a wild quarry that will be alarmed if it sees you, good anglers wear outdoor clothing in sensible muted colours. There is an industry dedicated to providing you with such apparel. It is all designed to keep you warm and dry.

Do you need waders? It depends where you are going to fish. Many small, still waters provide either small platforms or create spaces between bankside reeds and have strict 'No Wading' rules to minimize disturbance. All you will need are wellington boots to wade through wet grass. Do not forget, if you wear only wellingtons or other boots, you will need waterproof trousers if it rains.

On waters with shallow margins, or when fishing rivers, wading and waders are essential. Most waders are now made of breathable *Gore Tex* or similar material. Because they are comfortable to wear all day they are nearly all of the 'chest-high' variety. Some anglers use them as a partial substitute for waterproof clothing. They just need to be coupled with a short, waterproof 'wading jacket'. Almost no one buys thigh high waders any more. An average pair of chest waders costs around £300. Both cheaper and more expensive options are available.

There is one other piece of essential kit. When you hook a trout and play it into the shore it has to be directed into a *landing net* to lift it clear of the water. Any attempt to land a fish without a landing net will end in failure. Trout are slippery and lively. The hook hold is usually tenuous.

Landing nets come in many shapes and sizes. Still water fly fishers find one with a spike at the end of the handle that can be pushed into the ground very useful. The hoop and net can serve as a *line tray* to catch loose fly line and keep it out of the marginal undergrowth. A specially designed net of this sort will cost about £60. More everyday, easy-to-carry options cost around £30. They should be made with a fine, knotless mesh that will not damage trout that are returned to the water.

HEALTH AND SAFETY

There is a long list of hazards associated with fly fishing and enjoying the outdoor life. Fortunately, the actual risks are low and are avoided by common sense.

The biggest safety risk comes from slips, trips and falls. Wear sensible footwear, take care over difficult terrain and carry a mobile phone.

There is a small risk of eye damage from casting so always wear Polaroid sunglasses which, in any case, are an essential aid to see into clear water.

Most fisheries have shallow edges so the risk of drowning is low but wear a life jacket if you wish. There is a myth that if you fall into deep water your waders will fill with water and drag you down. In fact, waders and other clothing tend to hold air and keep you afloat initially. The right thing to do is not to panic and to turn onto your back. This gets your airways clear of the water. You then spread eagle your legs. You will float on your back and will be able to use your hands to paddle gently to safety. There are lots of films and videos that demonstrate this technique. Of course, a life jacket is an essential precaution if you are fishing from a boat.

The greatest health risk (both short and long term!) is from the sun. Wear sensible clothing and use sun block.

A FINAL WARNING

Learning to fly fish for trout will probably lead to a lifetime's passion. It will open a door to an endless variety of other angling experiences. Desires become obsessions and can seriously affect your life. You have been warned!

SUMMARY OF TOP TIPS

- Do not buy an expensive rod or reel.
- Invest in a good quality, two colour, floating fly line.
- Buy an intermediate sinking line too. Load it on a spare spool for your reel.
- Go one line weight up from the rating marked on the rod.
- Use a 3-metre tapered nylon leader with a metre of fluorocarbon tippet.
- All waters have 'favourite' flies. Use these patterns at first.
- Buy a beginner's rod, reel and fly line 'kit'. Get a discount!
- A fly fisher's waistcoat is a good investment.
- A landing net is essential.
- Wear sensible footwear and carry a mobile phone.
- Polaroid sunglasses have a dual purpose.
- Use sun-block.

2

ASSEMBLING THE EQUIPMENT
AND TYING KNOTS

Fly fishing is a simple process. You cast your fly onto the water and persuade a trout to grab it.

There is a difference between a field sport involving a wild quarry and a ball game like golf. When you play golf and your performance is less than perfect it is hardly a total failure. You can still enjoy your game. When fly fishing if your cast splashes down you will scare the trout away. If you cannot cast far enough the trout may not see your fly. You may choose the 'wrong' fly. You may retrieve the 'right' fly at the wrong speed or at the wrong depth so that it is ignored. Only 100 per cent will do. Anything else is failure!

Even if you succeed and hook a fish it still has to be landed. Every fisher has a tale of 'the big one that got away'. Sometimes the cause is a blunt hook, but often it is a broken leader or failed knot.

Of course, in both golf and fly fishing there is always a new hole to play or a new cast to make. But, at the end of a round of golf, you have at least played the game. If you cannot catch a trout, especially when others do, or one gets away, it hurts!

This chapter describes all the knots a fly fisher must be able to tie. It also gives some hints, and suggests some items to carry, that help bridge the narrow gap between failure and success.

ASSEMBLING A FLY ROD

Not long ago most fly rods were two-piece rods. Only the longest, such as salmon rods, were three-piece to make them manageable and to fit them into cars.

Today, nearly all trout rods come in four pieces. A 9 foot rod can be fitted into a rod tube which is less than 75 cm which will go in a suitcase. It certainly makes travelling a lot easier. It also means there is now a right way to assemble your new fly rod.

Before you put up your new fly rod for the first time lightly wax the male ferrules using a small piece of a candle. This will prevent the ferrules sticking. Nothing is more frustrating, when you are tired after a day's fishing, than finding you cannot take your rod apart.

Put the small piece of candle in a little plastic bag and put it in the pocket of your new waistcoat. It will probably last a lifetime.

Four-piece rods should be assembled by joining the tip and second sections first, then the final sections so that you end up with the butt section in your hand. The reason for this is obvious: if you do it in the reverse order you end up with the fragile tip in your hand and the heavy butt and rod handle swinging about in the wind. But beware. You still have to watch where the rod tip is. More rods are broken when they are being put together than when fishing. Do not swish it around. Not only can you bash it into something, you are putting an excessive strain on it when it is not throwing a line.

As you assemble the rod make sure the rod rings, through which the line will be threaded, are in line.

THE REEL

Fly reels are designed to be either left- or right-hand wind.

If you are right-handed you will hold your fly rod in your right hand and wind the reel with your left hand. Fly reels are designed to wind in the line when the spool is turned anti-clockwise. When wound in this direction, the ratchet on the reel is light and it clicks gently. When the reel spool is turned in a clockwise direction as line is removed when, for example, a hooked fish races away, a heavier ratchet or an adjustable clutch engages to help the fisher play the fish. Because most anglers are right-handed, the 'factory setting' for fly reels is left-hand wind.

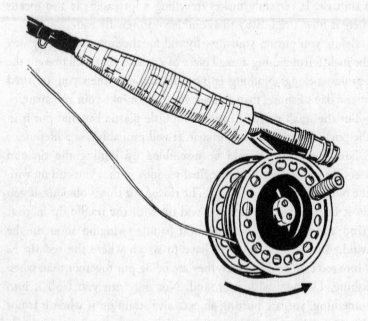

Fig. 7. Assembled rod and reel.

If you are left-handed, the setting needs to be reversed. All new fly reels come with instructions on how to convert them from left-hand wind to right-hand wind before use. It is usually a simple process involving turning over and replacing part of the ratchet/clutch mechanism. If it is necessary, change it before you start to put the line on the reel.

LOADING BACKING ONTO THE REEL

A backing line has to be put on a reel before the fly line. Backing line is cheap, braided nylon which is supplied on spools of varying capacity. You only need to put 50 metres on your reel. Backing line is a reserve if you have to play a trout that is powerful enough to run over 30 metres when hooked so that it pulls all the fly line from the reel. This never happens to most trout fishers. Everyone lives in hope!

The backing line serves another purpose. It builds up the diameter of the reel's spool before the fly line is wound on. There is a good reason for this. A wide diameter spool reduces the 'memory' coils in the fly line that inevitably occur when the line is pulled off the spool after it has been stored there for some time. Modern fly lines are all designed to have the lowest possible memory but it is impossible to remove it altogether. This is why all modern fly reels are designed with 'wide-arbour' spools.

Matching the size of reel and the fly line correctly means it should be easy to 'fill' the spool with the backing and the fly line. The reel maker usually specifies its capacity but the thickness of fly lines from different manufacturers does vary therefore a little trial-and-error may be required. If you find you need to build the reel diameter up a little before winding on the backing and fly line, use some everyday parcel string.

It is just as important to make sure the spool is not over-filled. What looks neatly filled, when the line is wound on carefully for the first time, can jam-up when the spool fills unevenly. A jammed reel is the last thing you want when you are playing a lively trout.

To wind backing line onto the reel it is easier if you first remove the spool of the fly reel from its cage to make it easier to tie the line to it. You must thread the end of the backing line through the cage before tying it onto the spool. Some fly reels have a specially designed *line guard* incorporated in the reel cage but if you are not sure where to thread it lay the cage on its back with the *reel seat* (the 'foot' that enables it to be attached to the rod) uppermost and thread the line through the lower quadrant of the cage from the left if left-hand wind or from the right if right-hand wind. This may seem elementary but it is common to see a beginner struggling with the wrong set-up. The end of the backing line should then be attached to the spool using a *Fisherman's Knot*. This simple knot secures the backing tightly onto the spool. You then put the spool back into the reel cage.

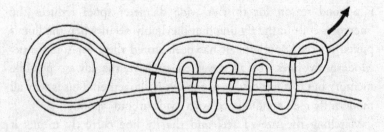

Fig. 8. Fisherman's knot. Used to attach end of backing line to reel spool.

Although the Fisherman's Knot is an easy knot to tie, it is as frustratingly difficult as any other knot when you try for the first time. Persevere! Soon you will be able to tie all the regular knots you use time after time with your eyes closed. Until you can do this you will find knot tying is easier if you hold the line against a dark background so that you can see what you are doing. It is also vitally important to coat each knot with your spit to lubricate it before it is tightened. For knots where two strands of line are being joined, or the knot is forming a loop, spit on them first. The surface tension keeps the two strands together.

To wind the backing onto the reel it helps to have a friend. He or she holds the backing line spool firmly on a pencil while you wind the length you need onto the reel. If you are on your own you will have to hold the pencil between your knees. You will quickly learn that having a friend certainly makes the task easier. Your aim is to make sure the layer of backing line is evenly layered on the reel spool and is kept tight enough to create a firm base for the fly line to follow.

LOADING THE FLY LINE

The next step is to put the fly line on the reel. This has to be done carefully.

A new fly line is packed in the factory in wide coils onto a two-piece plastic spool. It will be secured by small ties that need to be cut off. The correct end (i.e. the end of the 'running line') must be attached to the backing to ensure the line is correctly loaded on the reel. It is so easy to get this wrong that this end is usually labelled. Do not remove this helpful label until the end of the line is tied to the backing. Do not forget that this end of the fly line also has to go through the correct opening or line guard in the reel cage.

There are two possible methods of joining the backing line to the fly line.

The first is by using a *Nail Knot* as shown in Fig. 9. Because fly line is slippery, the knot is made more secure by tying a single overhand knot in the end of the fly line and tightening the Nail Knot snugly against it. The Nail Knot is most easily tied using a large darning needle rather than a nail. The free end of the backing can be passed through the eye of the needle to be pulled through the loops.

The knot between the backing line and fly line is one you may hardly ever see again. But, if the time you do see it is when the fly line is disappearing through the rod rings because you have hooked a giant trout, the last thing you want is for it to jam there. Therefore, after the Nail Knot has been trimmed, coat it with some *Zap-a-Gap* super glue which will give it a smooth, slightly flexible surface. This brand of super glue, which has been specially designed for anglers, is available from any fishing tackle shop or website. You must wait for the glue to dry before finally loading the fly line.

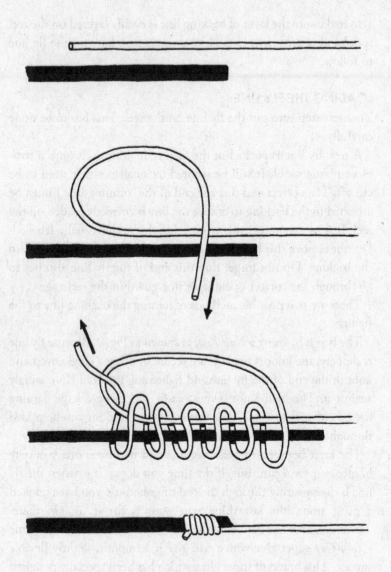

Fig. 9. Nail knot. Used to attach leader to tip of fly line or backing to fly line.

The other joining option is to fit a *Braided Nylon Loop* onto the end of the fly line and to tie the backing line to this using a *Tucked Half Blood Knot*. There are other knots but the Tucked Half Blood is one of the commonest knots used by fishers. It is secure and is easier to tie than many others.

Braided nylon loops sometimes come with new fly lines or can be bought separately, usually in packets of ten. You can also buy kits to make up your own. They make simple, non-bulky and effective joints.

To fit a braided loop 'sharpen' the end of the fly line by cutting across it at an angle and push the line up into the hollow braid towards the loop at its end. It can be awkward to do this as the end of the braid quickly starts to fray. The secret is to use the finger and thumb of both hands to ease the fly line inside the tube of the braid. (See figure 10 overleaf.) It is important to get the end of the fly line right along to the loop to avoid a 'hinge' of empty braid. Once the fly line end is in place, trim off any frayed end of the braid. Pass a short length of nylon monofilament line or other thread through the braid loop as the means of pulling it through a short length of plastic tube provided to form a neat seal over the junction between the end of the braid and the fly line.

Some makers will tell you this joint is now secure. Most experienced fly fishers dispute this! They always complete this set-up by adding a drop of Zap-a-Gap super glue to both ends of the plastic tube over the junction.

A Tucked Half Blood Knot is used to attach the backing line to the braided loop as shown. The Tucked Half Blood is the easiest and commonest fishing knot. It can be used whenever a line has to be attached to a 'loop' such as the eye of a hook, a swivel or a ring. Make four turns for Fluorocarbon line. Add a couple more if knotting Copolymer nylon as it is more 'slippery'.

The end of the line is 'tucked' into the large loop formed when tying the knot to increase its strength. Get into the habit of doing this every time.

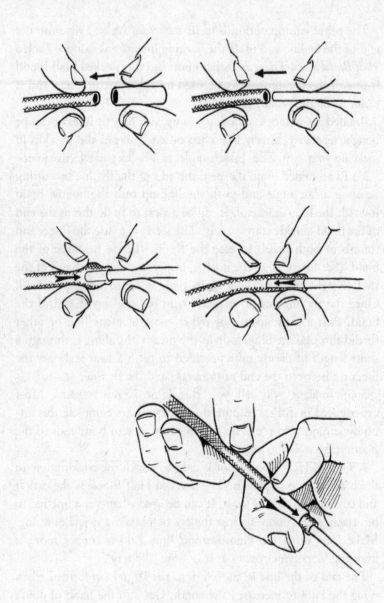

Fig. 10. Fitting a braided loop to the tip of a fly line.

Fig. 11. Tucked half blood knot. Used to tie fly to tippet.

Once the backing is joined to the end of the fly line it can be wound onto the reel. The coils in the new fly line must be unwound carefully as the line is transferred from its plastic spool onto the reel. It may seem tempting to remove the new line from its take-apart spool, throw it onto the floor and then to wind it onto the reel. This is a mistake because it prevents the 'factory' coils in the new line being 'unwound' and puts permanent 'twists' into the line which you may never be able to get rid of.

Keep the fly line on its spool, put a pencil through its central hole, get a friend to hold it firmly and wind it onto your reel so that the coils are unwound carefully. As long as it is loaded onto the reel properly the first time, the fly line will, from then, always lie in 'natural' coils.

Some line manufacturers advise you to dress their new line with some liquid 'plasticizer' before it is used for the first time. Modern fly lines are impregnated with a plasticizer to make them slippery so that they *shoot* further when cast. You pull the new line off the reel onto sheets of newspaper on the floor and then pull the line through a small piece of cloth soaked in the liquid plasticizer supplied. Leave it on the newspaper for an hour to dry before winding it back onto the reel.

It is wise to repeat this treatment every so often to clean the line and to replace the plasticizer which has leached out.

ATTACHING THE LEADER TO THE FLY LINE

Once the fly line is wound onto the reel, the leader has to be tied to the tip of the fly line.

A nylon or co-polymer tapered leader should be attached using a Nail Knot.

Nylon or co-polymer tightens securely over the tip of the fly line so an additional overhand knot at the end of the fly line is unnecessary. It still helps to smooth it over with Zap-a-Gap.

A Nail Knot is always the best option to join the thick butt of a tapered leader to the fly line because it provides the neatest join. If you put a braided loop on the end of the fly line, which may be supplied with it, any knot used to attach the thick leader end to the braided loop will be bulky and will tend to jam in the tip ring of the rod. Don't risk it!

USING A BRAIDED LOOP

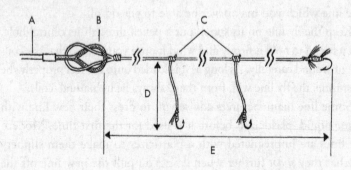

Fig. 12. Level leader with droppers.
A: Fly line. B: Braided loop. C: 3-turn water knots.
D: Length of droppers 15mm.
E: Length of leader from braided loop to tail fly 4 metres.

There are occasions when a tapered leader is not used and a fine, level leader can be attached to a braided loop which makes it easier to replace or re-tie. An obvious example is when the fly fisher wants to use more than one fly on the leader and attaches them by using short spurs at intervals along its length known as *droppers*. Such a level, fine, 3-metre-plus fluorocarbon leader is best attached to a braided loop on the end of the fly line using a simple *Loop-to-Loop Knot* as shown. The loop at the end of the leader is made using a *Three-Turn Loop Knot*.

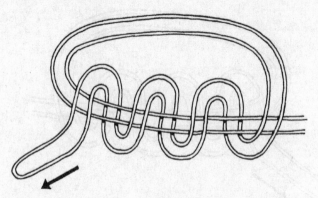

Fig. 13. Three-turn loop knot.

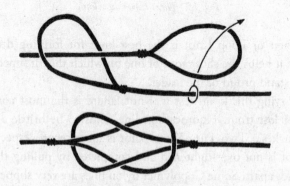

Fig. 14. Loop-to-loop knot.

TYING DROPPERS

The easy way to create droppers along a leader is to pick the position of the dropper and to tie a Three-Turn Loop Knot with a loop about 4 inches/10 cm long. Snip one leg of this loop close to the tightened knot and you have an 8 inch/20 cm dropper. Alternatively, you can cut the leader at the chosen point, lay the two strands of the cut leader together and join them using a *Three-Turn Water Knot* as shown. In practice, these two knots are identical.

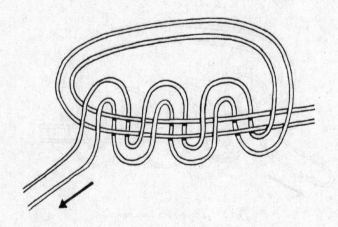

Fig. 15. Three-turn water knot.

A Water or Loop Knot is the best knot for forming droppers because it helps the short spur of line on which the 'dropper fly' is tied to stand proud of the leader.

After tying this knot, test it. Knot failure is the most common cause of lost trout. Fluorocarbon line tends to be brittle and for some makes a Two-Turn Water knot is more secure, especially if the knot is not over-tightened and completed by pulling the two long ends apart. Some Copolymer nylon lines are very slippery and a Four-Turn Water knot is even more secure.

JOINING NYLON OR FLUOROCARBON LINE

A Three-Turn Water Knot is also sometimes used to join two lengths of nylon monofilament or fluorocarbon line. It is not usually the best knot for this purpose because even when the free ends are trimmed tightly the knot puts a slight kink in the line that may initiate a tangle. A much better knot for joining two lengths of line is the *Full Blood Knot*. This is probably the commonest fisher's knot of all. It is neat and unobtrusive as well as being very strong. It is the knot you should use to join the end of a tapered leader to a short tippet.

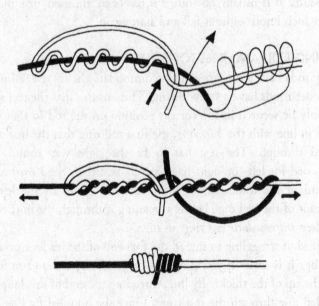

Fig. 16. Blood knot.

KNOT TYING HINTS

The Full Blood Knot is not the easiest knot to tie and it does take practice to tie it quickly and efficiently every time, especially when using fine leaders. There are special tools available to help you tie this knot if you cannot master it but usually it is best to persevere. Practise using relatively thick monofilament nylon until your fingers and thumbs learn what to do.

Fluorocarbon line is notoriously difficult to knot. One reason for this is that it is not naturally stretchy or slippery and sometimes does not tighten easily. If this happens it can be 'thinned' and stretched by the knot-tying process. This severely weakens fluorocarbon. All knots should, therefore, be lubricated by spit before they are tightened and they should be closely examined afterwards. It is usually obvious if it has been 'thinned' or kinked. Reject such knots without fail and start again.

PUTTING ROD AND REEL TOGETHER

All fly rods have a *reel fitting* to accommodate the fly reel. Almost all modern rods have a screw fitting. This ensures that the reel seat can only be secured in the correct position on the rod so that the reel is in line with the *butt ring*, the first rod ring that the line will be fed through. The reel has to be the right way round i.e. positioned for left- or right-hand wind. You then need to thread the end of the leader through the reel line guard or the lower quadrant of the reel cage before threading it through the butt ring and then *intermediate rod rings* in turn.

Instead of struggling to thread the fine end of the leader through the rings it is easier if you pull the leader off the reel and to fold over the tip of the thicker fly line, threading the end of this loop of doubled line through the rod rings. Once the doubled fly line tip is through the *tip ring*, pull on the butt of the leader to get the rest of it through the rings.

Reels come in different weights. The counsel of perfection is that when the fly line is through the rod rings the weight of the whole outfit should 'balance' around the point of grip. This usually means gripping the rod towards the front end of its short handle. If the reel and line are light-weight and the outfit feels 'tip heavy' some casting coaches will advise adding some weight to the reel or rod butt to achieve balance. Happily, this is rarely necessary today as it has become fashionable to use heavier, wide arbour reels despite the constant sales emphasis on ever lighter rods.

TYING THE FLY ONTO THE LEADER

Once the leader is through the rod rings the last task is to tie a fly onto the end of the tippet or leader. The commonest used, the Tucked Half Blood Knot, has already been described above.

There is another knot that is also useful. This is the *Turle Knot*, illustrated in Fig. 17. The reason this knot is useful is that it uses least line and produces less waste. You may think this does not matter because leader material, such as co-polymer or fluorocarbon, is relatively cheap but it is an advantage when you are tying a fly to a dropper. If you change the fly several times the dropper soon becomes too short and a new leader is required.

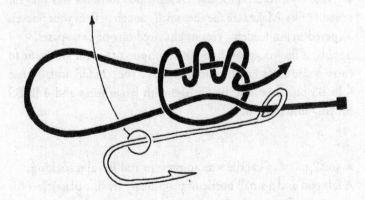

Fig. 17. Turle knot. Used to tie a fly to a dropper.
The knot is tightened by pulling the line through the hook eye.

The reason this knot 'saves' line is because the loop is tightened round the 'neck' of the hook behind the eye by pulling on the line in front of the hook, not on the free end.

OTHER TACKLE AND SOME 'MUST-HAVE' TOOLS

A great joy of fly fishing is how little heavy gear you need. But, that does not mean you need nothing other than your rod, reel, leader, flies and a landing net. There is a range of other bits-and-pieces that every fly fisher should carry. Not a day will pass when you will not be grateful you have got one or more of them. The following list will all fit into, or onto, the pockets of a fly fisher's waistcoat.

Every fly fisher has a slightly different 'must-have' list. The purpose of this one is only to get you started! Everything is available from every fly fishing shop or tackle dealer's website.

SPARE TACKLE

- A packet of braided loops – they may need replacing if lost or damaged.
- Fly boxes – two are probably enough, one for lures and one for imitative flies. Make sure they are small enough to fit in your pocket.
- Tapered nylon leaders. You might need one or two spares.
- Spools of fluorocarbon line for new tippets. You might want to carry some different breaking strains. You should usually use 6 lb BS but have 8 lb BS for use with larger lures and 4 lb BS for tiny imitative flies.

'STUFF'

- A small piece of candle wax to prevent rod ferrules sticking.
- A felt pad and a small bottle of proprietary fly line plasticizer for cleaning a floating fly line that gets dirty.
- A small bottle of proprietary fly line de-greaser for cleaning a sinking line.

- A neatly folded sheet of absorbent kitchen paper to dry floating flies that have become water-logged.
- A bottle of *Gink*, a proprietary material to help floating flies to float.
- A homemade paste of Fuller's Earth powder (available at any chemist's shop) and washing-up liquid. This is vital to sink leaders and tippets.
- A tin of *Green Mucilin*, a proprietary silicon material used to ensure the tip of a floating line, a braided loop or a leader will float if required.
- A tube of *Zap-a-Gap*. The super glue specially made for anglers... you never know when you'll need it!

'TOOLS'

- An engineered point to help open and untie the annoying overhand knots that regularly appear in leaders and tippets. It is vital to remove these knots as soon as they occur because fluorocarbon, co-polymer and nylon lines are all greatly weakened when such knots tighten. A 'chunky' engineered point is easier to handle than a needle which does the same job.
- A thermometer is worth carrying in the summer. If the temperature of a trout water is above 18° Celsius, trout become distressed and stop feeding. You might as well go home!
- A proprietary hook sharpening tool is an essential piece of kit. Hook points blunted by use or turned over by contact with vegetation are a common cause of lost trout. The best tool is a thin stick of carborundum that fits inside a pen-like case. It costs about £8.
- A *marrow spoon* to enable you to examine the stomach contents of a dead trout so that you can copy what is there. The Victorians invented the marrow spoon with a long narrow bowl used to scoop out the marrow from long bones. Marrow spoons were seized upon by the keen Victorian fly fishers as the perfect

tool to slide down a dead trout's gullet. Fly fishers are probably the only customers for marrow spoons today. You can buy a plastic one for under £2.

- A small pair of long-nosed pliers is essential to de-barb hooks. You just press the barb tightly to squeeze it into the hook. A de-barbed hook is a must if you intend to release the trout you catch. A pair of pliers comes in useful for other jobs too.
- A *Swiss army knife* as no fly fisher can have too many tools!
- A *priest,* the well-named tool that is used to knock a trout on the head if you are going to keep it for your tea. They come in various shapes and sizes. Prices vary depending on the material used. Anything is better than scrambling around to find a suitable stone or handy stick on the bank. Your quarry deserves a dignified end.
- A small pair of sharp-nosed scissors to trim flies or cut line. A good pair costs about £10.
- A pair of line snips is an even better way of cutting line and trimming the free end of line neatly after a knot has been tied. Most line snips also incorporate a needle point which is useful for poking excess varnish out of the hook-eye of a new fly. Snips cost about £7.
- A small pair of surgeon's artery forceps is the fly fisher's tool of choice to reach into a trout's throat to retrieve a deeply-swallowed fly. A trout has sharp teeth which damage your fingers! Fishing tackle dealers sell them for around £5 a pair.

OTHER USEFUL AIDS

- Always carry a small 'rag' or box of 'wipes' to keep your hands clean.
- A cheap pair of magnifying spectacles is very useful if you are over 50 years of age and have trouble focusing on anything within 25 cm of your eyes! Grown men have been reduced to tears by their inability to thread fine line through a hook-eye in

failing light when trout were *rising* all around them. You can get a pair from any chemists for £5.

- Polaroid sunglasses, including a cleaning cloth and strong case, are invaluable. They make a huge difference to your ability to see fish in the water by reducing glare. Getting them made to your prescription is a worthwhile investment. They also serve as eye-protection when casting or fighting your way through the undergrowth.

- A few small, sealable plastic bags always end up being useful to carry some new-found treasure home. You can steal them from the kitchen.

- A *bass* is essential if you are going to take a trout home. It is made from a permeable material and keeps a trout fresh if kept wet. Never carry trout in plastic bags... they cook! A bass costs less than £5 unless you want a deluxe version with a zip.

- A *fly patch* is a useful means of carrying spare flies outside their box. You must not put a damp fly straight back into your fly box or the hook will go rusty. Fly patches with a lamb's wool lining which clip onto your waistcoat are the answer. It is much wiser to buy one that folds over to protect the stored flies than an open patch. A pretty leather one will cost around £20.

'GIZMOS'

- Most fly fishers attach their snips and scissors to *zingers* or retractor strings which are pinned to their waistcoats. They allow you to use your tool on the end of the string which retracts neatly when you have finished using it. They save you trying to remember which pocket it is in and, more importantly, from dropping it into the grass! A good quality one which will not seize up the moment it gets wet costs about £10.

None of the above is essential but they are missed when you forget them. Going fishing fully equipped marks one of the stepping stones from beginner to expert.

SUMMARY OF TOP TIPS

- Assemble a fly rod by joining the tip sections first.
- Reverse a new fly reel to right-hand wind if you are left-handed.
- Match the fly reel to the line rating and 'fill' the reel with backing and line.
- Ensure the fly line and leader pass through the reel's line guard or the lower quadrant of the reel cage.
- Attach the backing to the reel spool using a Fisherman's Knot.
- Load a new fly line carefully onto the reel to 'unwind' its 'factory' coils.
- Join a tapered leader to the tip of a fly line using a Nail Knot. Coat it with Zap-a-Gap super glue.
- Put a braided loop on the tip of the fly line if you are using a fine, level leader.
- Use a Three-Turn Water Knot to make droppers in a leader.
- Attach a tippet to a leader using a Full Blood Knot.
- Tie a fly to the end of the tippet using a Tucked Half Blood Knot.
- Tie a fly to a dropper using a Turle Knot.
- Everyone has a 'must-have' list of spares, stuff, tools and 'gizmos'. You should be able to carry them all in the pockets of your fly fisher's waistcoat.

PART TWO

FLY CASTING

3
THE BASICS:
SIMPLE MECHANICS

At some time in pre-history a man or woman watched trout feeding on flies floating on a river's surface and had the bright idea of attaching a live fly to whatever they managed to use as a hook and line. They probably climbed a tree above the rising trout and lowered the fluttering fly to the surface. No doubt it was sipped down by an eager fish. This remains a good fishing tactic to this day. The limitation of this method is that it needs an overhanging tree. Perhaps the fly fishing rod was invented that very day!

Things had moved on by 1496 when the first book in English on fly fishing, written by Dame Juliana Berners, was published. She was using a tapered, flexible rod, with a tapered line attached to its tip and artificial flies made from feathers, because they were much more robust than the real thing.

Within a century Chinese writers were describing a reel with a line running through rod rings. Although we now use space age materials for the rod and line, the basic technology remains the same today.

HOW A FLY ROD WORKS

A springy, flexible fly rod and a thick, tapered line provide the force to propel a weightless fly over the water. Those who have studied elementary mechanics know that *Force = Weight x Acceleration*. The critical element in every cast is a flexing rod tip that 'accelerates-to-a-stop'. The rod's acceleration and the weight of the moving fly line create the force of the cast. The 'stop' transfers all this power into the unfurling line.

Achieving the optimum force depends on maximizing the tensile strength of the flexing rod.

A catapult helps us to understand what happens. Every schoolchild knows that when a catapult is loaded with a stone that is too light, even when the elastic is fully stretched, the stone will not go far. Conversely, if the stone is too heavy its weight will overwhelm the power of the elastic and the stone will fall at their feet. But, if the chosen stone is the 'right' weight it will fly to its target. Fly rods and fly lines are sized, labelled and matched to be 'right' for each other when the first 30 feet of the tapered line, known as its *head* is being cast.

CASTING TECHNIQUES AND STYLES

This book describes two casts. The *overhead cast* is used by most fly fishers most of the time. The *roll cast* is used to get the fly line in position to begin an overhead cast but is sometimes a useful cast in its own right. You need to be competent at both casts to get started.

CASTING IN EASY STAGES

The casting 'lessons' that follow divide the technique required into easy stages for the overhead cast and the roll cast.

You should treat them as a series of steps that need to be understood and mastered in turn before moving forward to the next. For each cast this progression, for those who have never tried to use a fly rod, may take an hour or more from beginning to end but some star pupils move through faster. What everyone needs to establish is a practice routine that can be used again and again to build up confidence and competence. It is also a routine that you can return to later when you need to refresh your skills or to sharpen them, perhaps before moving on to a new technique or when trying out new tackle.

Fly casting confidently, especially in difficult conditions, can seem like a distant dream for many beginners when they first try. It can be even more difficult for those who have tried to get started without the help of a professional coach and who have become confused by the contradictory advice they receive. So, whether you are an absolute beginner or a befuddled 'improver', here is the very first thing that you should do before you start to practise the casts described in the next chapter. The purpose of this exercise is simply to give you the confidence to use a fly rod and to trust your instincts.

THE GETTING STARTED EXERCISE

When learning to overhead cast for the first time the best location is a large, unobstructed grass field before moving onto casting over water. Roll casting is best learnt over water from the start.

Assemble your fly rod with the line and leader through the rod rings and tie a 5 cm loop of wool onto the end of the leader tippet using a Tucked Half Blood Knot. You need a fly or piece of wool on the end of the leader or else it will crack when you are practising. A piece of wool does not hook up in the grass.

Extend about two rod lengths of fly line on the ground in a straight line from the rod tip. Grip the rod handle so that your thumb is on top of the handle on the opposite side from the reel and pointing along the rod. Clamp the line tight against the underside of the rod handle with your index finger.

Now, without anyone telling you what to do, try this little test. Can you, using the rod, lift the extended line off the grass so that all the line is in the air and then can you put it back in exactly the same place and in the same straight line?

Don't worry if you cannot do it first time. Keep trying, walking backwards so that the line is straight out in front of you each time before trying again. Think of the rod as an extension of your arm.

When you have taught yourself to do this, there is a second test. Can you now lift the extended line off the grass into the air and,

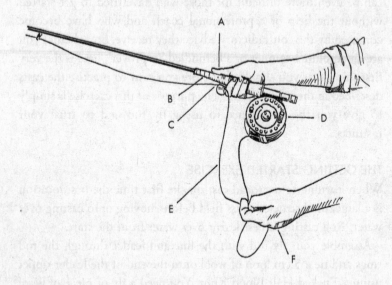

Fig. 18. How the rod and line are gripped.
A: Thumb on top. B: Handle. C: Line looped over index finger. D: Reel.
E: Fly line. F: Hand controlling loose line.

moving the rod backwards and forward above your head, keep the line in the air without it dropping and touching the ground?

You will immediately realize the secret is in *timing* the backward and forward movements of the rod *to let the line straighten out* behind you and then in front. See if you can manage a couple of back and forward casts without stopping.

Try to pass these tests before reading any further.

Almost everyone can succeed in these two exercises just by responding to the 'feel' of the rod and line. You might like to imagine you are driving a coach and horses and you have been given a whip that you need to use to gently touch the leading horses to encourage them.

This exercise should quickly teach you the two fundamental lessons of successful fly casting. The first is that it is impossible to lay the line back down straight in front unless it has been allowed to extend out behind you in a straight line. You have to 'time' how long this takes before you move the rod forward.

The second is that you can only keep the line in the air if you ensure it extends fully behind you and then in front of you and that it remains stretched tight by the moving rod once you have got it off the ground. If it goes slack, because of poor timing or hesitant backward and forward movements of the rod, you cannot stop the fly line falling to the ground in a heap! To start again you have to move backwards to straighten it.

Succeeding in these two basic exercises should give you all the confidence you need to learn to fly cast quickly. Do not worry if it feels difficult at first. It is like learning to ride a bicycle. You are very wobbly at first and then your 'muscle-memory' kicks in and you cannot understand what was so difficult. There is another parallel between bike riding and fly casting. Once you have learnt to do them, you never forget.

SUMMARY OF TOP TIPS

- The critical element of all casting is a rod tip that 'accelerates-to-a-stop'.
- All fly fishers need to master the *overhead* cast and the *roll* cast.
- Tie 5 cm of wool to the end of the leader when practising casting to prevent the line cracking like a whip.
- Use a practice exercise to develop 'timing' and the need to 'let the line straighten' between rod movements.

4
THE OVERHEAD CAST

In the world of fly fishing two distinct styles of casting and teaching have emerged.

'English style' overhead casting has its roots in the nineteenth century as part of the development of dry fly fishing on the chalk streams of southern England. Short, but accurate, casting with cane fly rods with 'middle-to-tip' action was required. The fly line had to be well elevated to keep it above the riverside vegetation.

Fly casting tuition of the day made lots of reference to clocks. The rod started at 'nine o'clock' and stopped at 'twelve o'clock' to create an overhead cast. The picture painted was of an elegant, upright caster and a vertical rod. Body movement was limited to the forearm.

An 'American style' developed in the twentieth century. Fly fishing in the sea off the Florida Keys became popular. This was done from skiffs, so there were no obstructions around, and it was important to be able to cast a long way. Stiff, light, tip-action rods made from carbon fibre were developed. The stance became open and the rod was held low, even horizontally, to get the fly line 'under the wind'.

This casting action was much more expansive, and involved the whole arm, so that the rod tip moved a long way. The free hand sometimes 'hauled' the fly line to increase its acceleration during the cast to achieve an even greater distance.

These two 'styles' of casting do look quite different. Their mechanics are not. The same 'rules' apply. Both 'styles' use the weight of a fly line to 'load' a tapered rod and then to 'release' its tensile strength. Both styles depend on timing the smooth acceleration of the rod tip needed to transfer the power of the straightening rod to the unfurling line.

The cast described below is 'English' in style. If you get it right by understanding how the cast works you will find it easy to convert to the 'American' way... hopefully, when you go to fly fish on the Florida Flats!

The overhead cast is the cast of choice for all fly fishers. This step-by-step guidance provides a learning process and a training/practice regime.

BEFORE YOU START – STANCE

Simply face the direction of the cast.

Most fly fishers keep their feet close together but some right-handed casters do find it easier to position their left foot a quarter of a pace in front of their right. The opposite is true if you are left-handed. What is important is to feel stable. Take your time if you are on an uneven or marshy bank!

Never forget you cast with your forearm, not your whole body. A firm stance helps keep your body and head still. This is what makes your casting technique look elegant.

BREAKING DOWN THE CAST

An overhead cast can be broken down into four elements – the *back cast*, the *forward cast*, *false casts* and *shooting line*.

The back cast is the most important. Overall, the technique depends on the initial execution of the back cast.

The following steps describe this casting sequence. Learn each one before moving on to the next. The sequence is also a practice routine and each element can be practised separately. Following the routine helps you understand common faults and problems. You can return to it in order to provide correction and reassurance.

It is impossible to watch yourself casting. This is why a coach helps. Some casting coaches resort to movie cameras, but it is also a great help to learn in a group and to watch other fly fishers.

Seeing what others do reinforces everyone's knowledge of good technique and the universal faults!

THE RULES

Before you attempt any overhead cast it is vital to understand there are three rules that must always be obeyed. Not heeding, or even understanding, these rules are common causes of frustration even among experienced fly fishers.

They are:

- **An overhead cast cannot begin unless the fly line is extended straight out from the caster and is on the surface of the water.**
- **The cast should start with the rod held horizontally in front of the caster.**
- **Throughout the initial back cast and all the subsequent forward and back casts the rod's movements should be in the same plane, i.e. the rod should NOT move backwards in one direction and aim forward in another.**

STAGE ONE: THE BACK CAST

The best place for a first lesson in overhead casting is a large, open field. The space enables you to walk backwards to ensure the line is extended straight out in front before attempting each new back cast.

Before you start, choose the direction you will cast so that any wind is blowing the line away from your body i.e. from left to right if you are right-handed. Face in this direction.

Pull line from the reel and walk backwards so that around 8 or 9 metres of line (i.e. approximately three rod lengths, most of the coloured 'head' of a two-colour line) is extended on the ground straight in front of you.

Hold the rod comfortably. All fingers should grasp around the handle with the thumb along the top (the opposite side to the rod rings) and pointing to the rod tip. You can control the fly line by passing it over your hooked index finger below the cork handle of the rod. Your finger acts like an extra rod ring directing the line onto the reel. More importantly, it provides instant control when you need to hold the line tight against the rod handle during casting and fishing. Your other hand is used to hold and to retrieve the line when casting and fishing.

Hold the fly line tightly against the cork handle with your index finger. The rod should be horizontal. Your hand will be about waist level. Now, try your first back cast.

Concentrate on your arm. Use your forearm only, with wrist stiff, to move the rod tip in a *smooth,* accelerating ninety degree arc. Watch the rod tip. The rod should come to a smooth stop when it is pointing vertically upwards. The rod handle should be close to your ear. The critical motion is a final, smooth *accelerate and stop* timed as a short, precise *power arc* over the last quarter of this cast. Remember a jerky stop is immediately transferred to, and kinks, the unfurling line. Experienced casters are able to achieve both a high rate of acceleration and stop smoothly. Beginners should favour smooth movement of the rod tip and line over speed.

At first, forget about casting forward. Let the line fall behind you. The big field allows you to re-position yourself for the next attempt. Get the back cast right before moving on to the next element. This takes practice! You will not get it right first time.

At first everyone tries to move the rod tip too fast, too soon. Start slowly! The rod tip has a long distance to travel. It must be at maximum acceleration when you stop. Achieve maximum velocity too soon and the rate of acceleration will be zero during the critical 'power arc'. Elegant casters look unhurried.

It also helps to imagine you are aiming to extend the line behind you above a 3-metre hedge. This should not be difficult. The rod is already adding almost 3 metres to your own height!

You will know you have got the back cast right when you *feel* the rod flexing backwards when the fly line has unfurled completely

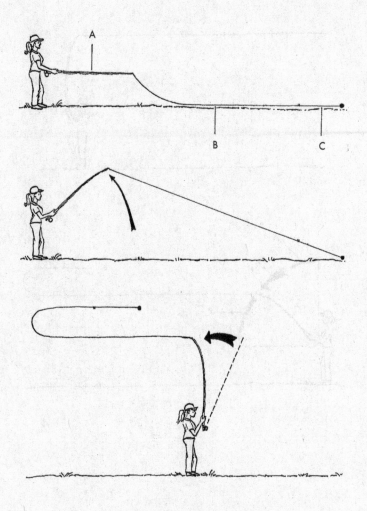

Fig. 19. Overhead cast – back cast.
Top: A: Start with rod horizontal. B: Fly line. C: Leader.
Middle: Start slowly.
Bottom: 'Power arc' to stop.

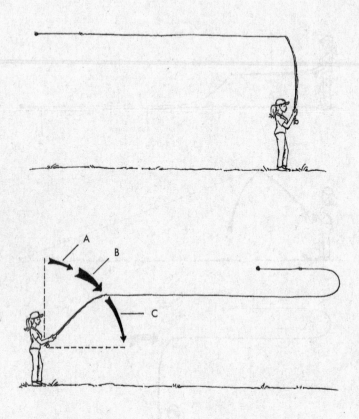

Fig. 20. Overhead cast – forward cast.
Top: Start when line is fully unfurled behind.
Bottom: A: Slow start. B: 'Power arc' to stop. C: Follow through.

behind you. Soon, you will feel this 'pull' every time. It helps if someone watches and encourages you. A qualified coach will get you there in a few minutes.

STAGE TWO: THE FORWARD CAST

The pull of the extended line flexing the rod backwards is the signal for the forward cast. The forward cast requires little effort after an effective back cast. After all, the tensile strength in the flexed rod straightens it and starts the forward cast even if you do nothing. Only a short, accelerating 'power arc' to another smooth stop is needed, so that the rod stops at about 45 degrees. Then, a gentle follow through to bring the rod back to its horizontal, starting position.

The aim is to ensure the line unfurls in a tight loop so that it fully straightens out in the air before the lowering rod helps to drop it gently onto the water or grass.

Do not try another cast at this stage. Just concentrate on achieving one strong back cast that results in a perfect forward cast which lays the line straight out in front.

STAGE THREE: FALSE CASTS

Everyone struggles to get started on a new cast. The reason for this is simple. The optimum length of fly line you need beyond the tip ring is the 8- or 9-metre head of a weight forward line. Getting this amount of line out in front is easy on a field where you can walk backwards but this is not an option at the waterside.

False casts are required. The purpose of a false cast is to keep the fly line in the air in order to extend the length of line beyond the rod tip before a final 'delivery' cast is made.

These casts are difficult. There is not enough weight of fly line beyond the rod tip to make the fly rod flex properly and to transfer its power to the extending line. This 'getting started' stage is when everyone suffers from tangles and other minor disasters.

You cannot start an overhead cast by pulling lots of line through the rod tip so that it lies in a heap in the water. The line *must* be extended in front of you before you can start an overhead cast. One way of doing this is to use a roll cast which is described in the next chapter but mostly fly fishers extend the right length of fly line through the rod tip by making a couple of false casts. Similarly, when you are fishing, you may want to retrieve your fly close to you before you re-cast and this will mean you will only have 2 metres or so of fly line beyond the rod tip. This too needs to be extended by false casting.

To practise false casts, start as if you were practising a back cast. The 8- to 9-metre head of the fly line should be extended in front of you on the grass or in the water. Use your 'free' hand, the left if you are right-handed, and keeping the rod horizontal, pull about 4 metres of the fly line through the rod rings so that it lies in loose coils at your feet. Keep hold of the line with this hand. Use the index finger of your other hand, which is holding the rod, to control the retrieval of this line and to ease out any kinks or tangles. From now on, only use your free hand to control the line.

When you back cast now you will notice that the 'pull' of a good back cast is weak because there is so little fly line beyond the rod tip. Let the line straighten behind you as before and make a forward cast aimed at the tops of some distant trees. Imagine them if necessary. 'Accelerate-to-a-stop' when the rod is about 60 degrees above the horizontal. As the fly line unfurls in front of you, 'open' the fingers of your free hand. The line will begin to move through the rod rings. A perfect false cast should take most of the 8- to 9-metre head through the tip ring. Use the light friction created by your free hand to keep the moving line 'tight'. *Before the line stops moving through the rod rings* grip it with your free hand to hold it tight and commence a new back cast. This back cast will be easier than before because the whole 8- to 9-metre head is the 'right' weight to load the rod.

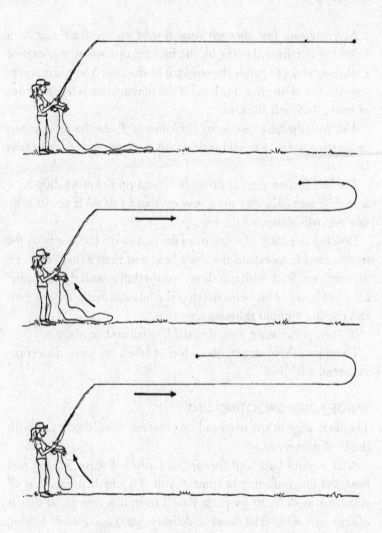

Overhead cast – false casts. The three-cast rhythm.
Cast One (top): Get line into the air.
Cast Two (middle): Release line on forward cast to get the head
of the WF line in the air.
Cast Three (bottom): Delivery Cast.   Release running line on forward cast.

Never release line through your fingers on the back cast. You should only release the line on the forward cast where you can see it moving and can gauge the strength in the cast. You must always stop the line with your free hand if the moving line is 'running out of steam' before it slackens.

Aim to keep false casting to a minimum. Even the most expert caster struggles to maintain their timing for more than three or four false casts.

The less fly line there is through the rod tip the more difficult it is to false cast. Always start a new overhead cast with as much fly line as possible beyond the rod tip.

Develop the habit of using one false cast to lift the line from the water, another to extend the line's head and then a final 'delivery' forward cast. Stick with this three-cast rhythm even if the false casts are not perfect. This helps develop the 'muscle memory' to repeat this rhythm without thinking about it.

If a cast goes wrong, stop. Let the line fall and start again.

There is nothing elegant about lots of false casts used in an effort to extend a fly line!

STAGE FOUR: SHOOTING LINE

The final stage of the overhead cast exercise is to 'shoot' line with the final delivery cast.

After a good back and forward cast you will have felt the pull from the line unfurling in front of you. To lengthen your cast all you have to do is to properly time letting this line go so that it 'shoots' out as the final forward, delivery cast is completed. Timing is vital. If you release the line from your free hand too early the unfurling line will sag and the cast will collapse. Ideally, the pull of the forward cast should trigger your fingers to let go.

Do not aim for the water's surface. By aiming for a point about 2 metres above the water you establish the right 'muscle memory' to achieve good turn over above the water, then a 'shoot' as the line is pulled through the rod rings and, finally, a gentle fall of the line and fly.

Aim for a strong, but measured, delivery cast that shoots about the same length of line on every cast. There is no point in straining to cast to the horizon every time. Settle for a comfortable and consistent distance.

If you do need extra distance, perhaps to reach a rising trout, do not be tempted to try more false casts or to extend more than the fly line head beyond the rod tip. Just put a little more effort into both parts of the final delivery cast. More line acceleration in both the backward and forward casts and consistent timing are all that is necessary. This is something you normally keep in reserve.

That is all you need to know. If you are lucky enough to be in your teens you will get the hang of overhead casting in double quick time. If you are older it will take longer! Going fishing gives you practice. Identify your faults and work to correct them. Elegance is as important as distance.

THE COMMON FAULTS

Teaching yourself means it takes a little longer to become a perfect caster than if you are working with a coach.

It takes time to master the basics. Try not to get frustrated. The problem is that fly casting is counter intuitive. For example, your head tells you all the effort should go into the forward cast because that is where you are aiming. But, because a fly rod uses its tensile strength to transfer its power to the fly line, a good back cast loads the flexing rod and the forward cast almost takes care of itself.

The commonest casting fault you will see is fly fishers straining for a stronger forward cast but failing, and often not even trying, to deliver a powerful back cast. Without this back cast, their overhead cast will always be a struggle.

There is a common myth that some fly fishers have weak wrists and that their wrists 'break' as they cast thus spoiling their overhead casts. They are even persuaded to buy devices to wear on their wrists which attach to the rod butt and act as a 'splint'. They need no such help. What they are doing is executing perfectly good back casts but after their 'accelerate-to-a-stop' power arc they fail to hold the rod *absolutely still* before starting their forward cast. Instinctively, they treat the rod, like a tennis racket or cricket bat and, unconsciously, seek 'backswing' to increase the power of the forward cast. The effect is catastrophic! The tension in both the flexing rod and the extending line is instantly lost. The source of power for the forward cast has gone.

This is what a good coach prevents from the outset. Unfortunately, there are fly fishers who have been struggling to cast well for years, and who have never sought help, and who just do not realize what they are doing wrong. Cruelly, the harder they try the worse they get. They put in even more backswing in a futile effort to beef up their forward cast.

The other common fault that needs to be avoided is a 'tailing loop'. This occurs when the leader and fly at the end of the fly line cross the body of the line during the backward or forward casts creating the risk of tangling. 'Tailing loops' are caused by poor timing of the application of power during the short power arcs, such as starting the forward stroke too early before the line is fully extended behind.

The same problem can also be caused by jerky movement of the rod tip. Only practice will 'smooth' the rate of line acceleration and the 'timing' of the 'power arcs'. Get them both right and the result is elegant casting... your ultimate aim.

DEALING WITH THE WIND

Wind direction and its effect on the line in the air is a critical factor in effective overhead casting.

If there is a head (or facing) wind the 'power arc' of the back cast should tilt forward into the wind to create a high back cast with a lower forward 'stop' and follow through. The aim is to shoot the line 'below' the wind. The power arc itself should *not* become longer.

If there is a following wind from behind, the opposite applies. The power arc should tilt backwards from normal, delivering a low back cast if obstructions permit. Then a high forward cast and a high 'stop'. Aiming into the sky takes advantage of the wind and aids a gentle delivery.

A crosswind which takes the fly line in the air away from your body is welcome as long as it is not too strong. A crosswind in the other direction is a curse!

You will sometimes see a long bank on a fishery that is deserted by right-handed fly fishers just because there is a right-to-left wind blowing along it. It makes casting difficult as the line in the air is blown into your body whenever your timing is less than perfect.

There are two simple solutions. The first is to practise to cast with a backhand style. If you are right-handed, you angle the rod to your left and cast over your left shoulder. This puts the fly line in the air to the left, and down wind, of your body.

The second option is to learn to cast left-handed (or right-handed). This sounds like an awesome prospect to most people. In practice, it is actually remarkably easy to become an ambidextrous caster. It is not the timing of the casting that you will struggle with, it is getting the fingers of your 'wrong' hand to hold and to manipulate the fly line comfortably.

Do persevere, it is a great skill to master and will serve you for a lifetime.

CHANGING THE DIRECTION OF A CAST

The overhead cast allows for easy changes in the direction of the cast of up to 60 degrees. As you move your feet to face in the new direction, simply keep the rod tip low and sweep it slowly sideways to point in the direction required before lifting off the straight line (always essential) and casting normally. Try to ensure the line in the air is on the downwind side of your body and over the appropriate shoulder.

If you require a really wide change of direction you should use two or three separate false casts, moving the feet and rod tip to face the new direction with each cast. The critical rule of overhead casting is that the rod must stay in the same vertical plane for each backward and forward cast.

By far the commonest fault when changing direction is to make a back cast in the direction of the extended line and then a forward cast in the new direction sought. This creates a large, unwieldy loop. The fly or leader usually tangles with the body of the line as it unfurls.

SUMMARY

OVERHEAD CASTING – THE 'RULES'

- An overhead cast cannot begin unless the fly line is extended straight out from the caster and is on the surface of the water.
- The cast should start with the rod held horizontally in front of the caster.
- During the initial back cast and all the subsequent forward and back casts the rod's movements should be in the same plane, i.e. the rod should NOT move backwards in one direction and aim forwards in another.

THE BACK CAST

- Start with the rod held horizontally.
- The rod is an extension of the forearm, keep the wrist stiff.
- Start slowly! Watch the rod tip.
- Smoothly accelerate to a stop.

THE FORWARD CAST

- Keep your hand absolutely still after completing the back cast.
- Wait until you feel the extended line flexing the rod.
- Do not move your hand backwards!
- Cast forward smoothly, accelerate to a stop at 45 degrees.

FALSE CASTS

- Ensure the line to be 'shot' is in loose coils and not tangled.
- Aim the forward cast at a point 6 metres above the water.
- Do not release the line too early.
- Grip the shooting line with your free hand before it slows down
- Get into a three-cast rhythm.

SHOOTING LINE
- Do not let go too early when releasing the line.
- Aim for a point well above the water surface.
- Aim for a comfortable distance. Do not strain for a long cast each time.

AVOIDING COMMON FAULTS – HINTS THAT HELP
- Try rotating the rod to the right (if right-handed) by nearly 90 degrees to place the reel behind the wrist. This 'feel' of the reel helps to prevent 'back swing'.
- Alternatively, (if right-handed) move the thumb a little to the left from the top of the rod and point the index finger along the right side of the handle. The wrist is stiffened by an extended finger.
- Grip the rod more tightly just before the 'stop' position is reached. This helps to achieve the smooth stop required *and to hold this position until you start the forward cast!*
- Cast by lifting the forearm directly in front of your nose to prevent the back cast going beyond the vertical.

FINALLY GETTING IT RIGHT!
- The line lifts from the water without disturbance (if it is splashy the initial acceleration is too fast and needs to be slower and smoother).
- The line unfurls in a tight loop over the top of the rod.
- You have 'muscle memory', perfect timing and a three-cast rhythm. You'll never forget how it's done!

5
THE ROLL CAST

The overhead cast is the cast that most trout fishers use most of the time but there is another cast that every trout fisher must learn. This is the roll cast. The first rule of overhead casting is that the fly line must be straight out in front before the cast can start. The roll cast is how to get it there.

When first pulled off the reel the fly line will be in loose coils below the rod tip. A roll cast is the 'getting started' cast. A roll casts lifts this loose line into the air and, with a single forward movement, casts it out straight in front on the water. Now, the overhead cast can begin.

There are many other occasions when a roll cast is necessary. For example, if a trout is missed or lost, or if a cast goes wrong, the fly line ends up in a mess on the water. It has to be straightened out before the next overhead cast. Or, a sunk-line has to be lifted out of the water and laid out straight on the surface before it can be cast again.

The aspiring trout fisher will read and hear a lot about fly casting and various fancy casts. At first, remember that only two casts, the overhead and the roll, must be in every fly fisher's armoury. It pays to learn to do them well. Understanding how and why they work prevents endless frustration later.

For some, skilful fly casting becomes a passion. For the rest, it is simply the means to an end. Being able to cast accurately and in all conditions is the start of learning to fly fish. Nobody ever caught a trout while casting. How the fly is 'presented' after it is in or on the water is what counts! Do not become obsessed with casting. Understanding the quarry is more important than being able to exhibit the use of the tools.

Learning to roll cast is essential. If the fly line is not extended out in front of you it is fatal to attempt an overhead cast. You must do a roll cast to extend it.

The roll cast is not the easiest cast because there is no back cast and flexing rod to aid the forward cast. But, as there will be many occasions when you end up with the fly line in a heap in front of you, you will get plenty of opportunities to practise it.

There is another valuable use for the roll cast. It gets a line out when there are obstructions behind. The fly line hardly goes behind you when you roll cast.

The roll cast must be practised over water, not on a field. Pick a spot where there is plenty of room around you and a minimum of vegetation to catch the line. A small, low jetty is ideal.

STANCE

Before you try a first cast, pull line off the reel so that it lies close to your feet. Then, hold the rod point very close to the surface of the water in front of you and waggle it. The effect of the surface tension 'holding' the line enables you to get out about 5 metres of line onto the water in front of you safely and easily. To extend these loose coils out into a straight line in front of you a roll cast is needed.

Later you will be able to roll cast the whole head of a weight forward line but do not start with too much to do.

Check the wind. You must have a crosswind that takes the line away from your body. A left-to-right crosswind is essential if you are right-handed. Do not attempt your first roll cast if there is a crosswind in the opposite direction!

Keep your feet close together and face in the direction you want to cast.

GRIP

Hold the rod well up the handle, thumb on top.

MECHANICS

The roll cast is a two-stage cast. The first is lifting the 5 metres or so of fly line into a large loop beside you by raising the rod. The line forms a capital 'D', of which the rod is the straight line. The tip of the fly line must remain in the water as an 'anchor'.

The second stage is the 'power arc' to roll the 'D' loop through the air in the desired direction.

STAGE ONE – THE LIFT

While you carefully *watch the end of the fly line* in the water, lift the hand holding the rod up close to your ear so that the rod tip is pointing backwards around 30 degrees from the vertical. Cant the rod over a little away from your body. The line will follow the movement of the rod tip. Wait for the end of the fly line to *stop moving*. This tells you the 'D loop' is fully formed.

You can now see what this 'lift' has done. The end of the fly line is in the water to the downwind side of your body creating an 'anchor' that will help tension the line. The belly of the line is hanging from the rod tip to form a 'D loop' to provide weight. The roll cast is all 'power arc' from this standing start.

STAGE TWO – THE POWER ARC

The cast is a short forward movement, keeping your wrist stiff, which moves the rod tip from 30 degrees behind the vertical to 30 degrees in front. Once again this cast is 'accelerate-to-a-stop'. To ensure the maximum rate of acceleration at the 'stop' it is vital to start slowly. It is much better to sacrifice some final acceleration rather than to move so fast initially that the rod is no longer accelerating when you smoothly stop. The result should be a loop of line rolling forward well above the water which then drops gently to the surface.

This roll cast 'power arc' takes practice. The movement is higher up than an overhead cast, but it still depends on rapid acceleration

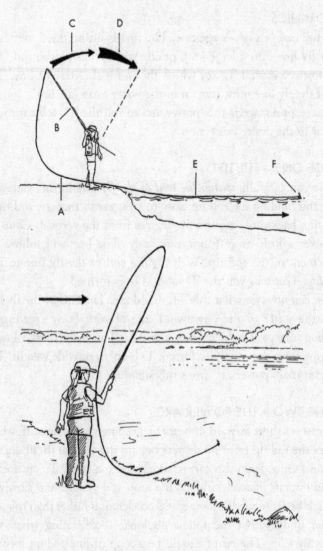

Fig. 22. Roll cast.
Top: Side view. A: 'D' loop. B: Rod. C: Start slowly.
D: 'Power arc' to stop. E: Line in water. F: Fly.
Bottom: Rear view. Arrow shows direction of wind.

from a slow start, a stiff wrist and a little downward movement of the whole arm.

WINDS

You must take account of the impact of the wind.

If you are right-handed the 'easiest' wind is one that comes from your left-hand-side. The reason is obvious. This wind keeps the fly line, including the rolling loop as the cast is made, away from the body so that there is no danger of being struck by the fly. The 'anchor', where the tip of the fly line is on the surface of the water, has to be in line with your body or to the right. Keeping the line to the right is the reason the rod is canted over a little towards the right before the power is applied to make the cast.

If the wind is coming from the right a roll cast *must not* be made on the right-hand-side of the body. If you tried to roll cast in such a wind both the 'D loop' and the rolling loop would be blown into your body as the cast is made and an untidy tangle is inevitable.

There is a solution. You have to form the 'anchor point' and the 'D loop' on the left-hand, downwind side of the body. You can simply swap hands and cast with your left hand. It is surprising how easy it is for most of us to do this. Alternatively, cast 'back handed' over your left shoulder keeping the rod in your right hand. The hand position, and the application of power, must be just the same as if the cast was on the right. It takes a bit of practice.

If the wind is coming from directly behind its effect is to collapse the 'D' loop thus reducing the 'weight' available to make the cast. To counter this, as the lift is made, the rod tip has to make an exaggerated movement backwards into the wind to get into a start position closer to the horizontal than usual. The cast should be made the moment the fly line tip stops moving before the wind further collapses the 'D loop'. The secret of making this cast is to ensure that, although the 'power arc' starts further back, it remains as short and precise as before. The effect is to aim the cast high. You will find the following wind aids and smoothes out the delivery after the essential 'stop' as you lower the rod gently towards the water's surface.

A facing wind from directly in front creates the opposite problem and mirror image solutions. The facing wind tends to increase the 'D loop' but then to collapse the rolling loop when the cast is made and to blow it back into your face. Counter this by not pointing the rod as far backwards at the start of the cast. The wind will ensure the 'D loop' is formed. In effect, the starting point for the power arc has been moved forward. The arc the rod tip follows should still be through 60 degrees to a smooth stop, but the effect is to drive the rolling loop forwards and downwards as if you are aiming to force it under the wind. It works!

CHANGE OF DIRECTION

A weakness of the roll cast, in contrast to the overhead cast, is that large changes in direction of a second cast cannot be made after a first one. The maximum possible is about 30 degrees, but 20 degrees is easier.

A small change of just a few degrees is not a problem. Your feet should be moved to face the new direction. Note the wind direction. A move to the right when there is a wind from the left may need an exaggerated pointing of the rod to the right and some extra cant to the right before the cast is made to ensure that the fly line 'anchor' is to the right of the mid line of your body.

If a bigger change in direction is required, but still within the 30 degree maximum, a more exaggerated movement of the rod tip will be required to form a 'D loop' on the downwind side of the body.

For example, the most difficult change of direction would be when the wind is coming from your right and you want to move to face to the left. The rod, held horizontally, has to be moved from pointing at 45 degrees to your left across the front of the body until it is pointing at 45 degrees to the right. The line will follow. The rod tip is then moved back along the surface of the water to its start point. This will straighten out the line to form a single loop of line on the water in front of you. Lifting the rod into the 'back hand' start position with your right hand close to your left ear will form the 'D loop' to the left of your body. The tip of the line will now be to the left of your body where it will form the 'anchor'. Wait until the tip of the line stops moving, then cast.

In short, any significant change of direction demands a similar exaggerated movement of the rod tip across the body and back again to ensure that both the 'anchor' and 'D loop' is formed on the downwind side of the caster. It takes practice!

SUMMARY

ROLL CAST – THE RULES

- The roll cast is essential to straighten out line which is loosely coiled beyond the rod tip before an overhead cast can be made. Every fly caster must be able to roll cast.
- Lift the rod so that the reel is level with your ear and the rod tip is pointing upwards and behind you at about 30 degrees from vertical.
- Wait until the 'D loop' is fully formed by watching for the tip of the line to stop moving.
- Start slowly! *Accelerate-to-a-stop* with the rod pointing upwards in front of you at about 30 degrees from vertical, i.e. a movement through 60 degrees.

ROLL CAST – HINTS THAT HELP

- The roll cast power arc starts with the hand holding the rod up level with your ear. The forearm moves downwards, not forward. Aim to get the loop unfurling high above the water.
- The 'power arc' of all single handed fly casts depends on the rod being an extension of a stiff wrist/forearm and on the rod tip 'accelerating-to-a-stop'.
- Always aim at a point a metre or so above the water as an aid to improving/shortening the 'power arc'.
- There will be a length of fly line beyond the rod tip which is the optimum distance to roll cast because it is long enough to create an 'anchor' point and to provide enough weight in the 'D loop' to flex the rod. Practise with this length, marking the line if necessary, before trying to roll cast further.

- A good roll caster is able to 'shoot' line by releasing it as the rod 'stops' and the line rolls out.
- Change direction by two or three roll casts, each one a 20 degree change or less, rather than attempting the large change in one cast.
- The roll cast is also used when trees, bushes or another obstruction behind the caster prevents an overhead cast.
- On many fisheries there are places where trees or bushes prevent overhead casting and anglers avoid these spots. The trout are not disturbed there and are often close to the bank and in easy reach of a short roll cast.
- If new casters practise hard, their casting skills will rapidly improve as their 'muscle memory' kicks in. It is like learning to ride a bicycle and will never be lost. *If this does not happen, there is something fundamentally wrong with your technique and you need to consult a qualified angling coach.*

6

GIVING THE FLY LIFE

This book aims to get you started at fly fishing, not just casting. Of course, the first step in becoming a good fly fisher is learning to cast. Skilful casting means you are able to get your fly where you want, and that more fish will see it without being alarmed. But, whether they take the fly or not depends on the fly pattern you show them and what you do with it after the cast... how you retrieve it!

There are plenty of expert fly casters who are not very good fishers. They are more passionate about casting than in understanding trout behaviour and being able to make the right fly irresistible to a vulnerable fish. There are even more poor casters who have all the other skills. Guess who are the most successful anglers?

The guidance in the previous chapters aims to set you on the path to becoming an expert caster. What follows aims to make you an expert fly fisher.

LINE CONTROL IS VITAL

When casting, 'control' of the fly line using your 'free' hand and the index finger of your rod hand is important. Your index finger is able to trap the line against the rod's cork handle. It should form a 'hook' below the handle that the line can be slotted onto. The free hand can grasp the line and should be in constant contact with it. The hands work together to control the line to keep it tight. Everyone quickly learns that if the line becomes slack, even for a moment, the tension between the flexing rod and the moving line is lost and the cast 'collapses'.

It is just as vital to keep control of the fly line after the cast has been made. The index finger on the rod hand is able to clamp the line tight if a trout takes the fly so that the hook is set. The free hand 'retrieves' the fly line to keep it tight and to keep you in touch with the fly. The speed and nature of the retrieve dictates the movement of the fly. This element of the overall *presentation* of the fly is usually the secret of success.

WHY DIFFERENT RETRIEVES?

There is another obvious reason for keeping the line tight using the index finger and the free hand after a successful cast. The moment the fly lands in the water it may be grabbed by a hungry trout. You do not want to lose the fish because you have not tightened the line and are unable to feel the 'take' or to react.

At some time, everyone suffers the indignity of catching nothing while fishing alongside someone who, although using the same fly line and fly, hooks fish after fish. Something about the way they retrieve and move the fly through the water is what makes the difference.

The following chapters on trout behaviour and on tactics give advice on how to retrieve the fly in order to induce a take or to ensure that the fly behaves like a natural insect or other prey.

But first it is important to understand the basic retrieves and the terminology used in fly fishing literature to describe them.

KEEPING A 'TIGHT LINE'

Imagine you make a perfect cast and the fly line and leader unfurl in a straight line before dropping gently onto the water. The rod follows through as the line lands and you point the rod tip *down the line*. The fly line is in the crooked index finger of your rod hand and any loose line behind it is being grasped by your free hand. In this perfect, tight line situation, if a trout engulfs your fly as it lands, and they often do, you will feel a firm tug on the line. All you need to do is to instantly trap the line against the rod with your index finger so that the tight line drives the hook point home. Then, you can gently lift the rod tip and start to play a well deserved trout. It is important *not to attempt to 'strike'* by lifting the rod tip. Fly rod tips are very thin and flexible so a strike is unlikely to provide enough strength to sink the hook. It is much better to depend upon the tight line anchored against the rod handle by the index finger to drive the hook home.

A more likely scenario is that your cast is not perfect and there is some slack line between the rod tip and the fly on the end of the leader. Your first job is to hook the line over the index finger below the rod handle and to use the free hand to retrieve line *quickly* until it is straightened out in front of you. This puts you *in touch* and able to respond if a trout takes your fly but *only if your rod tip is pointing down the line.*

FINDING THE RIGHT DEPTH

Before you start to retrieve further line you have options. The first is how long to delay the retrieve to allow the fly to sink to your chosen depth. If the fly is heavy, perhaps it has a gold bead head or has some lead in its dressing, it will sink quickly. Be prepared for it to be taken *on-the-drop* by a trout as it sinks. If this happens you will feel a sharp tug. You just need to clasp the line tightly with your index finger. Then you can lift the rod to cushion the first struggles of the hooked trout.

If you are using a weighted fly you need to have a good idea of how fast it sinks (you should watch and time how fast it sinks in a large glass of water at home). Make a decision on what depth you want it to get to and measure it down by counting. Naturally, this is the depth you think the fish are! Once the fly is down to the required depth you start to retrieve. Mostly, you have to guess the 'right' depth. You can start by counting to five after your first cast, ten after your second and so on. Keep experimenting until you get a response.

If the fly is not weighted and especially if it is dressed with buoyant furs and feathers, it may be trapped in the surface film or sink very slowly. If you are using a floating fly line, you will inevitably retrieve it very close to the surface. You may have to change to a heavier fly if the fish are not feeding close to the surface.

Some fly patterns are *dry flies* or *emergers* which are designed to float on or in the surface film. These are usually fished *static* simply because natural flies and those emerging from their larval form do not move when they land on, or rise to, the surface. Moving dry flies look unnatural and are likely to be rejected by, rather than to attract, a trout.

But, if there is a breeze blowing towards you, or you are fishing against the current in a river, it will move the floating fly so the fly line will still have to be retrieved using your free hand just to keep you in touch. If a side wind is blowing it will 'bow' the line which may need to be *mended* by flicking its belly back against the wind to keep it straight in an effort to prevent the fly from being towed round by the bowing fly line. This will not work for long. To keep the fly 'static' in a crosswind or in a river demands constant re-casting.

Dry fly fishing is great fun but during most of the trout season you are more likely to be using *wet flies* designed to be fished below the surface of the water. These flies are tied using natural fur and soft hackles that sink easily through the surface film. Many imitate insects during the sub-surface stage of their life-cycle. Many insect larvae or *nymphs* are highly mobile. The correct retrieve recreates this movement. This is what an alert, feeding trout is waiting for and what triggers a take.

Garish *lures* may not imitate any living thing but how they move persuades a trout to chase and take them. When the water is cold in the spring, it may be a slow, continuous movement close to the bottom that eventually induces a take. In the heat of the summer, speed near the surface may be the answer while in the autumn a static white lure that imitates a dead, coarse fish fry may be what is needed.

In short, there is a lot to think about before you decide how and at what depth you retrieve your fly. And, there are endless ways in which a wet fly or lure can be retrieved. Fly fishers develop highly personal styles. They can be distilled down to the following headings.

'DEAD SLOW AND STOP'

This retrieve, as indicated above, is required to imitate natural insects or other trout prey that do not move naturally.

Obvious examples are flies that imitate a terrestrial insect such as the familiar Crane Fly or Daddy-Long-Legs which is blown onto the water from surrounding fields. This can be a spectacularly successful fly in September. When the wind blows 'Daddies' onto the water they are helpless to escape. Trout instantly recognize this temporary, seasonal bonanza and will patrol a lee shore hungrily sipping down each one they find. The problem for the fisher, as noted above, is preventing the artificial fly being dragged around unnaturally behind a fly line that is being moved by a crosswind. Trout often ignore moving artificial Daddies or swirl at them without taking them properly.

Some wet or sinking flies are also best fished static.

A good example is the *buzzer*. In the UK these are the commonest of the freshwater insects that live out most of their life-cycle in large or small still waters.

Each spring, as if a switch has suddenly been pressed, huge numbers of buzzer pupae of a particular species rise slowly to the surface together where they emerge quickly into flying adults. The pupae cannot swim. When they all decide to emerge from the lake bed, an air bubble forms under their shiny outer skin so that they float slowly to the surface. Trout are able to cruise around and to mop them up at their leisure. These feeding trout learn to avoid an artificial fly that moves quickly or horizontally.

An artificial buzzer usually consists of nothing more than appropriately coloured thread wound round a hook which is given a couple of coats of varnish or super glue to imitate the natural pupa's shiny cuticle. These flies are very effective when the naturals are on the trout's menu.

One way to keep them static is to put a floating plastic indicator called a *bung* (there are many different makes) on the leader close to its junction with the fly line. The bung acts as a float which suspends the stationary buzzer below it. Chapter 14 describes all the tactics used to catch trout feeding on buzzers.

'STOP/START'

Other insects and creepy-crawlies on which trout feed all year round do not move or swim about at a constant speed or in straight lines. Most are invisible for most of the time as they hide on the bottom or cling to water weeds. Their presence, if they are disturbed, is revealed to a trout by their movement as they try to regain cover. It is this movement that provokes the feeding response.

If you can actually see a trout, whether in running or still water, the best ploy is to cast your fly so that it sinks down to the fish's depth, as close to its nose as possible, before raising the rod tip a few centimetres to 'lift' it and imitate escaping prey. This often persuades the trout to grab the fly. This is an *induced take*.

On most still water trout fisheries the trout are out of sight or difficult to see clearly, but the same principle applies. After casting, let the fly settle or sink to your selected depth and then retrieve line with your free hand to ensure the fly darts forward and then stops. A take can come the moment the fly moves or it may come a few seconds after it stops. There are endless variations on this theme.

The movement can be very short, only about a couple of centimetres, or a longer *draw*. The gap between movements can be just a second or so, or extended – perhaps while waiting for a visible fish to swim into range!

'FIGURE-OF-EIGHT'

Forty years ago still water trout fishers were reminded that the insects and other creatures their artificial flies imitate swim with jerky movements. The angling press of the day recommended that they used their free hand to retrieve their fly line by twisting their hand to gather off a hand's width of line with each movement. The effect is a continuing stop/start retrieve of 10 cm of line at a time until you are ready to re-cast. The speed of retrieve can vary from very slow to as fast as possible.

This 'figure-of-eight' retrieve remains very popular and many fly fishers use it nearly all the time. Its other advantage is that, by holding the short loops of retrieved line in your free hand, it does not fall to the ground where it may tangle with the undergrowth.

The same effect is achieved by simply retrieving the line in 10 cm-draws with the free hand with the line passing over the index finger of the hand holding the rod. And, doing it this way is far less likely to lead to a repetitive sprain injury!

'LONG DRAW'

The majority of still water trout are *not* caught on flies that imitate insects or other natural food. They are caught on *attractor* flies, or *lures*, which incorporate bright colours and synthetic materials. Lures are a magnet to aggressive or inquisitive trout. While lures do catch trout when retrieved using the same retrieves and at the slow speed used for imitative flies it is often better to use a faster, but continuous, retrieve produced by a long draw of a metre or more of line using the free hand. It also helps to let the rod tip rise and fall in concert with the steady draws of the free hand. This irons out the stops and starts and retrieves the lure at a constant speed from the start of the retrieve until you have to re-cast.

THE 'ROLY-POLY'

Recently, in recognition of the effectiveness of fishing a lure at a constant, non-stop speed, the quirky 'roly-poly' retrieve was invented. You stick the rod butt under your arm and use both hands, one after the other, to smoothly retrieve the line and lure at your chosen rate. It often out-fishes any other method of retrieving lures.

There is more on achieving success using lures in Chapter 7 on Trout Behaviour and in Chapter 10 on lure fishing tactics.

THE CORRECT LEADER LENGTH

The optimum length of leader and tippet from the end of the fly line to the fly is around 4 metres. A steeply tapered, 3-metre nylon leader is a great help to novice casters. It aids turnover of the final forward cast. But, the more tippet that is added to the leader to lengthen it, the more difficult good casting becomes. The leader and tippet, unlike the fly line, have no intrinsic weight to provide forward momentum. Even the most expert casters struggle with leaders longer than 6 or 7 metres. They are difficult to turn over, tangle easily and snag repeatedly on bank side vegetation. So why does anyone use long leaders?

The answer is obvious. The tip of a fly line is thick and can easily scare a wary trout. And, if you are fishing with a floating line in 2 metres of water or more, and you want to get your fly down to the bottom, you do need a long leader. The leader with a fly on the end of it does not hang down vertically as it sinks. The tightened leader forms a wide arc from the floating tip of the fly line. It must be tight, and about three times the depth of the water, if you are to feel takes 'on-the-drop' and keep in touch with the sinking fly.

Inevitably you have to compromise. Keep the leader to the minimum length, over 3 metres, that you can get away with. Never attempt anything longer than 6 metres or so. It also helps to use slightly heavier flies which provide a little weight to aid the final turnover. Flies with bead heads are often ideal. Another tip is to use flies dressed on heavier wire hooks. You may not be able to buy such flies but a friend who ties flies may help. This tiny amount of extra weight in the fly has the added advantage that it will also help to get the fly down towards the bottom more quickly and this, after all, is probably the reason for trying to cast with a lengthened leader. But, beware, there is a limit to the extra weight that can be added to a fly before this advantage turns into a nightmare. Very heavy flies and light fly rods are incompatible!

If the water you are fishing is more than 3 metres deep and you really do need to get down to the bottom, you have no option other than to use a sinking line and a comfortable length of leader.

FISHING WITH MORE THAN ONE FLY ON THE LEADER

When you are getting started at fly casting you are strongly advised to stick to one fly only on the end of your leader and tippet. It is wise advice. Soon, however, the tactics you need to catch a trout cry out for more than one fly to expand your options. These are explained in detail in the chapters that follow.

For example, when fishing with buzzer pupa imitations you want to explore various depths from the bottom up to close to the surface. When using a floating line this means using a long leader. You give yourself, and the feeding trout, more chances if you have buzzer pupa imitations at intervals on the leader.

Additional flies are tied onto a leader on 10–15 cm droppers. These are made by tying a Water Knot in the leader, as illustrated in Chapter 2. You might limit yourself to one dropper at first but many experienced fly fishers use two or three to achieve more options.

When using droppers and additional flies it is vital to remember that they must be tied on your leader/tippet within a distance that is less than the length of your rod. Flies *do not* pass through the tip ring of your fly rod! There is nothing more embarrassing than playing a trout hooked on the tail fly and finding the top dropper firmly hooked in your rod's tip ring with the distance between the two flies making it impossible to net the fish.

When using droppers you do not need the recommended 3-metre tapered nylon leader. You can tie a 2 to 4 metre fluorocarbon leader to the end of the flyline which includes two droppers. This would present three flies at intervals of approximately one metre.

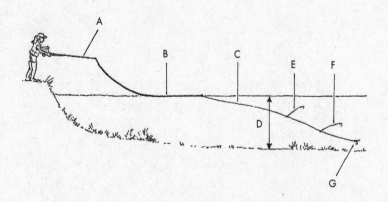

Fig. 23. Fishing a floating fly line with droppers at different depths.
A: Rod. B: Floating fly line. C: Leader. D: 2 metres.
E and F: Droppers and flies. G: Heavy 'tail' fly.

The most important thing to remember when fishing with dropper flies, no matter what set-up you choose, is to ensure that the heaviest and most streamlined fly is in the tail fly position. This aids casting and leader turnover. It also helps to ensure that the flies fish from a straight leader at the desired depths. Putting a heavy fly in any other position on the leader is a recipe for disaster!

In the next chapter you will learn that the other vital use of dropper flies is to combine imitative flies with buoyant *Booby* lures to ensure they can be fished effectively at the selected depth. There is more on fishing with Boobies later.

SUMMARY

RETRIEVING THE FLY

- Always use your free hand to tighten the line between the rod tip and fly as soon as you have cast. You cannot feel a *take* if the line is slack.
- Decide how deep you want your fly to sink unless you want it to fish on or near the surface. Let it sink before retrieving. Expect a take 'on-the-drop' as it does.
- Decide on the right 'retrieve' each cast. Be prepared to vary it. Do not become an automaton, always casting and retrieving at the same speed and depth.
- If what you are doing is not working... try something else!

USING LONG LEADERS AND DROPPERS

- 3–4 metres is optional, 5–6 metres is the maximum when 'getting started'.
- A *lightly* weighted tail fly aids turnover of a long leader.
- Dropper flies provide valuable options.
- Droppers should be tied in the leader using a Water Knot.
- The gap between the tail fly and the top dropper must not be greater than the length of the rod.
- Your casting ability should dictate the total length of the leader and the number of droppers used.
- Use droppers only when tactics demand them.

PART THREE

FLY FISHING TACTICS

7

ESSENTIALS OF TROUT BEHAVIOUR: WHAT MAKES IT TICK?

A trout is shaped like the fish every child draws. It is streamlined and torpedo shaped. It is built for speed and forward movement.

Rainbow trout have bright silver sides, a white underbelly and a camouflaged blue back. They are difficult to see from both above and from below and are 'designed' to live at all depths.

Brown trout, as their name suggests, are often darker in colour but their other physical characteristics are similar. A number of other species of trout are sometimes stocked in still waters and rivers in the UK but rainbow trout are by far the commonest.

All trout have a mouth that is huge in comparison to body size and they have sharp teeth. They can, and do, eat prey of all sizes. They have big eyes too and can see in all light conditions.

Like most fish, trout have ears and can hear noise which travels easily underwater. They also have a unique organ called the lateral line which means they are sensitive to vibrations. This is a 'sense' that we do not share so it is easily forgotten. It is the reason why fly fishers have to learn to move 'softly'. It also explains some trout behaviour that the fly fisher can exploit.

In summary, trout are fast moving, predatory fish that hunt by sight. They are not specialist feeders. If they can they will avoid dirty, cloudy water in favour of clear water with better visibility.

INTERNAL ORGANS AND PHYSIOLOGY

BUOYANCY

Like most fish, trout have an obvious air-filled swim bladder. This organ provides buoyancy to counteract their 'weight' in the water.

This means that trout do not have to expand energy maintaining their preferred depth. It also may explain why they are reluctant to change the depth at which they have chosen to swim (perhaps it is uncomfortable as pressure changes?) and is why presenting an artificial 'fly' at the correct depth is a vital part of fly fishing. There will be much more on this.

TEMPERATURE

Fish do not maintain a constant body temperature like mammals. This means changes in water temperature have a strong impact on them. All trout species have their origins in cold water. They survive happily in ice-covered lakes. High UK summer temperatures, especially in shallow, still waters can easily become too high for trout. This is why many small trout fisheries close in July and August when water temperatures can rise to a lethal level (which is 27° Celsius for rainbow trout). The scientific evidence shows that trout's activity and appetite reach a maximum between 10–19° Celsius but fall off rapidly above this. Thus, wild trout put on most weight in spring and autumn if there is plenty of food available.

Salmon fishers carry thermometers to get an indication of when salmon will rise. Summer trout fishers need one to see when fishing is a waste of time!

DIET

A trout has a large stomach and short gut which also indicates its preference for a varied, high protein diet. All sensible fishermen examine the stomach contents of any trout they have killed using a *marrow spoon* or by dissecting their catch. Obviously, this is the best way to know what the fish is feeding on.

Carnivorous fish like trout do not feed all the time. Brown trout are particularly active at dawn and dusk. Rainbow trout are more constant feeders if some food is available but also seem more likely to stop feeding entirely if stocked into unproductive, acidic upland waters where prey species are scarce. However, like all predators, trout are 'hard wired' to take full advantage of temporary excesses of food such as insect *hatches*, vulnerable shoals of prey fish or *blooms* of *Daphnia*, the water flea, a tiny shrimp-like crustacean.

In fact, for all trout, whether wild or hatchery reared, high protein *Daphnia* is always their food of choice if it is available.

The aquatic insect species that spend part of their life-cycle in fresh water are of particular interest to the trout and the fly fisher. Most species have evolved so that they *emerge* or *hatch* into flying adults at the same time. This does not mean only one hatch per year. It usually means hatches at a particular time of year, perhaps over a few days when conditions are suitable, but always in big numbers. Such a mass hatch protects most of them, whether the immature underwater stage or the winged, mature adult, from predation. But, a hatch also triggers a trout feeding frenzy as they attempt to take advantage of a short lived bounty. Such a *rise* of trout should make them very vulnerable to the fly fisher. Sometimes it does, but every fly fisher experiences the frustration of trout rising all around and finding nothing in their fly box that will tempt them. There are two reasons for this. The first is simply that an angler's fly may be only one among many and is not one of those engulfed. The second, and more usual reason, is that the fish are responding to very specific physical characteristics of the hatching insect or to one aspect of its behaviour. For example, they may be taking them at a very precise depth or particular stage in their change from one form to another. The result is that a 'wrong' artificial fly is ignored.

Such puzzles are one of the joys of fishing. It does not feel so at the time!

OBSERVATION AND RECORDS

The lesson for everyone getting started is this. Anglers who study their 'home' waters will learn how the trout behave year in, year out. They will record when insect hatches occur, what weather conditions suit and where and when the trout shoal. There are always surprises, but the effort to study trout behaviour and to find the 'right' fly, the best place and the critical time is always rewarded in the end. But, be warned, it is a road to obsession!

Luckily for the beginner, you do not need to do all this work yourself. Most fly fishers are friendly and, especially if encouraged by praise, are happy to share their secrets. Do not be shy about asking.

LET'S GET REAL!

It would be wonderful if every trout fishery was populated by wild trout born in a pristine feeder stream. Your local water will not be so blessed unless you live in a very wild place.

Everyone else fishes in commercial, well managed fisheries. Almost all are stocked with rainbow trout. These fish are specially reared for release in such fisheries so, unlike their fellows destined for a supermarket shelf, they have well developed fins and tails, bright silver colouring and usually weigh around 1 kg/2 lb. Some even bigger trout are stocked for anglers too. Do not imagine they get bigger by natural feeding. Rainbow trout do grow on in rich, large lakes and reservoirs but not in heavily stocked small fisheries.

The theme of this chapter is simple. If you are to persuade a trout, whether wild or reared, to take your fly you cannot ignore the following facts on trout behaviour.

LEARNING LESSONS

There are many trout anglers who never make progress beyond their 'getting started' skills because they fail to observe trout behaviour. They enjoy fishing, and good luck to them, but they never develop the hunter's instincts, a respect for their quarry and an understanding of the where, when and how of trout reactions to

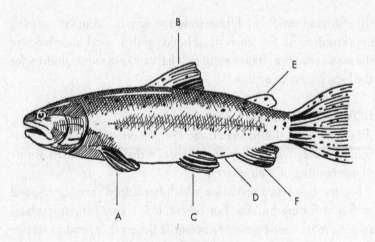

Fig. 24. Rainbow trout.
A: Pectoral fin. B: Dorsal fin. C: Pelvic fins. D: Vent.
E: Adipose fin. F: Anal fin.

their mysterious underwater world. The joy of this knowledge, the result of never-ending inquisitiveness and experimentation, is the essence of fishing. This know-how exposes the 'vulnerability' of the fish. The 'art' of trout fishing is acquiring the full range of skills to exploit this weakness. But beware! Every time you think you have 'cracked it' you will soon be humbled by another trout!

Sometimes trout feeding behaviour is obvious and even the most unobservant fly fisher can see a trout rising with a visible splash, perhaps to take a newly hatched floating fly. But, the really successful fisher will not only see this rise, he or she will have anticipated it. Their experience, past observation and experiments will have taught them when and where such feeding occurs and what artificial fly is needed to fool the feeding trout. This knowledge cannot just be gleaned from books. Every stretch of water is unique. The trout's environment changes constantly with the changing season, and from season to season. Trout are amazing opportunists. All fly fishers must build up their local knowledge of the water they fish. These trout will have unique vulnerabilities for the local expert to exploit.

HOW DO FISH THINK?

All experienced, skilled anglers can describe one or two days in their fishing careers when they learnt lessons that shaped their future understanding of their quarry.

For some, it was a revelation which has helped them to respond to future fishing puzzles. For others, it is a tiny insight, perhaps relating to just one corner of a favourite fishery that remains forever their secret.

No matter how frustrating they are, and even if impossible to catch, trout do not have human-like intelligence. They do not see a morsel of natural food or an artificial fly and say to themselves, 'Oh, I recognize that and it is good to eat.'

Scientific experiments reveal they have more mechanistic responses to potential food or other stimuli but it is wise never to underestimate their powers of sight, smell and taste or the speed at which they learn what to avoid. Their ability to respond to vibrations is a sense we cannot easily comprehend.

In short, it helps to assume that a trout can see, and *feel* the movements of a pinhead at a distance of 3 metres. Another startling way of looking at this is that, if you cast your fly 20 metres out into a clear lake and you retrieve it to your feet, your fly has been seen by every trout in 120 square metres of the lake. Now ask the question, 'Why did I get no reaction?'

BASIC TACTICS

There are libraries of books on complex fly fishing tactics. Read them all. Each one will teach you something about how to catch

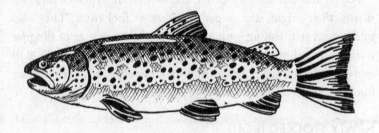

Fig. 25. Brown trout.

trout. But, at times, no matter how much knowledge you acquire, you will still fail. Frustration is part of fly fishing! The advice in this book on tactics will not prevent failure. It does aim to answer the basic 'what works?' questions on fly fishing for trout. It should be a foundation on which you can build new skills. More important, perhaps, it provides insight too into why success can be elusive.

Beginners are not always well served by popular angling books. Many are written by experts for experts, often about a narrow slice of the fly fishing world. They can confuse as easily as they inform. Other books do target the learner but concentrate on the technical skills of casting. There is a suggestion that trout give themselves up as long as you can get a fly in front of them. They do not!

Even worst, some writing paints a romantic picture of trout, blessed with human-like desires, picking and choosing the wild prey they feed on. These authors belittle modern fly fishers, and the stocked rainbow trout everyone catches. This is a sad throw-back to some Victorian attitudes on fly fishing. Ignore them! Today's experts happily use a wide variety of flies, including lures and attractors, and not only those which imitate natural food.

Today, the thinking fly fisher knows that all types of flies, no matter their origin, are needed at times to fool trout. They also understand that fishing with a lure is not just a matter of slinging it out and hauling it back until a trout grabs hold. In fact, the skill and expertise needed to catch trout on lures, especially with sinking lines, is considerable.

NEWLY STOCKED TROUT

Trout from a fish farm have spent their life cruising round a small pond into which pellets of food are regularly dispersed by an automatic feeder. They probably also get an occasional treat when a hapless flying insect makes the fatal mistake of alighting on the surface of the pond. These trout never forget being fed on pellets. On some stocked trout waters the fish are sustained by pellet feeding during the winter. Throwing in a handful always causes a feeding frenzy. There are some trout waters which are opened for coarse fishing with bait in the hot mid-summer months. Surviving trout learn to avoid some coarse fishing baits, such as maggots, but are always suckers for pellets!

Trout newly stocked into a fishery find their constant supply of pellets suddenly ends. They are inquisitive fish and soon get hungry.

Many are quickly hooked and caught as they investigate the variety of anglers' lures and flies that they see. They are often very easy to catch. Any fly attracts them. Its colour, size and movement may not matter at first. The stomach contents of newly stocked trout demonstrate this. Alongside half digested pellets from their last meal in the trout farm you will find twigs, leaves, and bizarre litter such as cigarette butts.

This naivety does not last long.

In small, heavily stocked waters where newly introduced trout quickly see a wide variety of flies and lures, and especially if catch-and-release is practised, they soon learn to avoid the fly fisher's best efforts. Even if every trout caught is killed it seems that the survivors learn what to avoid, perhaps by seeing the distress of the trout that does grab a fly or lure. Of course, these newly stocked trout also see more 'natural' food, if stocked in a fertile lake, than they have ever seen before in their lives. They quickly learn to eat it... and feeding frenzies occur... if large numbers of insects hatch at once or if there are large shoals of coarse fish fry to prey on.

Trout which adapt to natural feeding may be slow to learn to avoid the angler's imitation of their new food source but, as many frustrated fishers know, these feeding fish can learn quickly how to select the 'real thing' and to reject the fly fisher's offering.

Rainbow trout stocked into waters which are biologically poor and where there is no natural food not only learn, after a short time, to avoid anglers' flies they also seem to totally shut down their feeding behaviour. They seem to become moribund, impossible to catch and survive on their fat reserves before eventually losing weight and condition. The fishery owner has to re-stock some naive new fish for the anglers to catch even though there are plenty of survivors of earlier stockings.

WILD TROUT
Only those fly fishers who live in, or visit, wilderness areas such as the north of Scotland, wild areas of Wales or the English Lake District enjoy the privilege of catching native wild brown trout in lakes and rivers.

Do not get over-romantic about wild trout. Obviously, no wild trout grows to a good size without developing natural cunning but they often live in 'hungry' environments and they can feed greedily and without much caution when food is available. These are great waters for beginners.

Other wild trout lakes and lochs have poor spawning, ample feeding and produce a small population of trout that grow big if they are not over-exploited. Individuals from such a small population can be hard to find and hard to catch but they are not impossible. Work out where and on what they are feeding. Then you just have to get the right fly, at the right time into the right place!

FINALLY

There are three basic questions. Where are the trout? When should I fish? How do I persuade a trout to take my fly?

There are some answers to these questions that apply everywhere. But, never forget that every trout is uniquely 'programmed' by where it lives. Your own observations and experience count for just as much as the advice and tactics in this book.

Aim to become a local expert!

SUMMARY

ESSENTIAL FACTS

Trout

- Are opportunistic feeders.
- Adapt their diet to the 'local' prey available.
- Are *not human* and do not react to food like us!
- Have amazing eyesight.
- Can 'feel' movement.
- Are inquisitive when newly stocked but rapidly learn what to avoid.
- Become 'selective' in their reactions to an abundance of prey.

SMALL TROUT FISHERIES – PROS AND CONS

- The downside to fishing for stocked trout in smaller still waters is that the water may become too hot in warm weather, especially in mid-summer, and the fish may become distressed and impossible to catch. Another is that trout that have been in the water for some time may learn to 'avoid' all artificial flies.

The upside of small, stocked trout fisheries is that the trout
- Tend to be in reach.
- Do respond to rises of natural food.
- Are particularly vulnerable to floating terrestrial flies that fall on the surface.

And, of course, commercial trout fisheries are regularly restocked with naive, inquisitive trout.

Trout behaviour is complex but remember:

- The reaction, in small still waters, of newly stocked trout to their new environment explains why fishing there can be either a feast or a famine.
- Being able to cast a fly is not enough to fool most trout. You need the right tactics too. This is where 'getting started' gets really interesting.
- 'Romantic' fly fishers ponder, 'Why do trout behave as they do?' It is a good question, but the successful, more 'technical' fisher worries more about 'what works?' than 'why?'

8

WHERE?

Finding trout fishing is easy. In all parts of the UK there are small trout fisheries that are perfect for getting started. Small fisheries are usually well-stocked. This makes them easier than big lakes and reservoirs. The questions may be the same but the solutions are not so hard to find. This is why small waters are the best place to start if you can.

Problems start on arrival. Do I fish here? Or over there? Should I try deep water or shallow? Is it better to fish close to the shore or out in the middle?

The answer is to think like a fish. The question is, 'If I were a trout, where would I want to be?'

There is no advice about finding a small still water where you can fish for trout in this book. There does not need to be. Wherever you live or visit in the UK you will find a trout water nearby. On page 224 there is a list of established, well-managed trout fisheries provided by the Stillwater Trout Fisheries' Association. Even in the most far flung corners of Scotland, Wales and Ireland, alongside lochs or small lakes containing wild brown trout, there is usually a 'commercial' fishery or two that is well stocked with rainbow trout and available for the cost of a day ticket.

All around the British Isles there are large reservoirs and lakes that are open for trout fishing. Many are managed by the water companies that provide public water supplies. Their qualities as trout fisheries vary a lot. Some are 'natural' wild brown trout waters; others are heavily stocked with rainbow trout and maintain fleets of fishing boats. The best, such as Rutland reservoir and Grafham Water, which are managed by Anglian Water, have become international fishing destinations for fly fishing enthusiasts. They regularly host international 'loch-style' fly fishing competitions where competitors fish in pairs from drifting boats.

Despite their popularity, these waters do not provide easy fishing for beginners. A rule of thumb is that 70 per cent of the trout will be in 30 per cent of the reservoir. This can make them hard to find, especially in 3,000 acres or around a 10-mile shoreline. Boat handling and casting from a drifting boat on (most) windy days can be challenging! The average catch for a fishing session is only 3 or 4 trout, about half that achieved on many small fisheries.

Beginners who try to tackle these waters without lots of help from a guide or friend are often overcome by the difficulties. But, if you persist, the rewards and sense of achievement are huge.

The tactics that follow apply to all trout waters, big or small, and an effort is made to unravel some of the differences and challenges.

Only the best natural, wild brown trout fisheries are run as commercial enterprises by their owners. Most of the rest are run economically by local clubs. They are no worse for that and some are regularly stocked with brown trout. Some huge Irish 'loughs' such as Corrib and Mask and some large Scottish lochs are famous trout fishing destinations. None provide simple fishing for beginners and it is irresponsible to go afloat on these wild, often dangerous waters, without an experienced 'ghillie' or guide. Like big reservoirs, it may be best to aspire to conquer these exciting places after you have 'got started'. Chapter 16 gives more advice. Some natural fisheries are 'easy' because good spawning and nursery areas produce a large, and hungry, population of small wild fish. Others are 'hard' because a lack of spawning areas restricts the population. Of course, the best wild trout waters have adequate spawning areas, productive feeding and low exploitation.

Such waters are rare, highly prized and protected. Find one if you can!

Small rainbow trout fisheries are much easier to create. Top quality rainbow trout, bred for the rod-fishing market, are available and survive in almost any small water. It is easy to ensure that the stock in the lake provides the fishing experience desired. Some fisheries are heavily stocked with 'standard' sized fish up to 2 lb/1 kg, while others include, or concentrate on, bigger fish to attract those fly fishers who are desperate to catch a monster.

WHAT WATER SHOULD YOU CHOOSE?

Everyone eventually gravitates to the waters that suit them best and provide the challenge they seek but when you are getting started you should look for three things.

The first is help and support. It is fine to go to a wild, isolated fishery if you are with an experienced companion to teach and support you. It may be easier to find a friendly, commercial rainbow trout water where beginners are carefully nurtured as future customers and there is someone around to provide encouragement, good advice and a helping hand.

Secondly, it is uniquely difficult to get started at fly fishing because, until you are a competent caster, the development of other skills has to go on hold. Find a fishery where long distance casting is not necessary, there is shelter from strong winds and where there is plenty of space to cast. Well positioned platforms can be a boon. Once you have developed expertise you can gravitate to other waters where you will have plenty of chances to 'fight the weather and foliage'.

Finally, choose a beautiful location! In such places you will learn there is more to fly fishing than catching trout. Our world is awash with buildings, busy roads and noise. Fishing makes more sense in a wild place... even if it is only a well-designed oasis close to the urban sprawl.

THERE ARE LOTS OF PLACES TO FISH IN THIS LAKE... WHERE SHOULD I START?

This is a vital question.

Elinor Trout Fishery near Kettering is often the venue for the final of a national competition for small water trout fishers who have qualified by winning a match on their local fishery. The competition is fished over two days and the water is 'pegged' so that competitors have to fish 20 metres apart. There is a draw to allot their starting 'peg'. At the end of each half-hour everyone has to move round 10 pegs and then they fish at their new peg for the next half-hour and so on. The intention is to prevent a free-for-all for the 'hot spots' and to give everyone a fair chance.

Every year there are three 'pegs' that are always the best places to fish. There will be one or two others that also do consistently well over the two days but these vary from year to year. There are other spots that almost never produce a fish although there is no obvious reason for this. Of course, weather conditions also play a part but the overriding lesson is that fishing in the 'right' place in any water plays a huge part in your success.

At Elinor, all the regulars know where the best pegs are. They always start fishing at these places and there is a friendly competition to get there first in the morning. Despite the 'pressure' on these 'hot spots' most continue to give up trout after trout. It often pays to follow the crowd!

While some 'hot spots' are constantly good, others are obviously related to prevailing conditions. You need to work out the 'hot spots' at your local fishery. Why are they so productive? I give some hints below.

And, do not forget that fishery owners usually want you to succeed, so just ask them for help.

One of the problems of big reservoirs and lakes is that fish may choose to leave shallow shorelines for deeper water that is out of reach for all bank fishers. Their only chance of success may be to fish from a dam or other spot giving access to deeper water. Boat fishers have access to deeper water but wild conditions may make it challenging to present their flies effectively if trout are feeding a long way down.

DEPTH IS CRITICAL

The most important element of where to fish is finding the 'right' depth to fish your flies at. Trout do not like to move from their chosen depth. There are lots of reasons why trout choose to swim at a particular depth. It could be temperature, in response to food supply, the light level or for many other reasons. And, of course, these will change through the course of a day. But if trout are cruising close to the bottom you should assume that they will not respond to any fly that is fished close to the surface. Similarly, if they are close to the surface, they will ignore a fly that is below them.

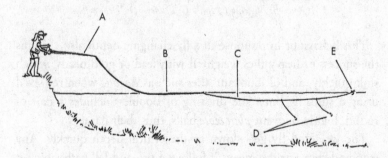

Fig. 26. Fishing a floating line with buoyant tail fly holding up droppers.
A: Rod. B: Floating fly line. C: Leader. D: Droppers and flies. E: Buoyant tail fly.

A fly that gets down to its chosen depth is more likely to evoke interest when it stays at this depth long enough for the trout to see it. Experience, and your own observations in crystal-clear waters, will soon convince you that trout often follow a fly for a long way. Often, what finally induces a *take* is the fly changing depth, typically at the last gasp of the retrieve as you are preparing to re-cast. Presumably, the trout sees the fly suddenly moving upwards, is reluctant to follow, and has to grab it or to leave it!

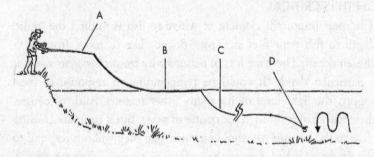

Fig. 27. Fishing a floating line with a weighted fly and a 'sink-and-draw' retrieve.
A: Rod. B: Floating fly line. C: Leader. D: 'Heavy' fly.

This behaviour in response to a fly changing depth also explains the success of heavy flies weighted with lead or gold beads, which sink quickly, and of 'buoyant' flies such as *Boobies* when retrieved using a sunk fly line. The dressing of Boobies includes a pair of round, highly-buoyant *plastazote* balls, thus their name!

The weighted fly gets down to the critical depth quickly. Any stop-and-start retrieve means it follows a rise-and-fall path which is likely to induce a take.

Similarly, a buoyant Booby fished behind a sinking line which has been allowed to sink to the depth required helps the retrieve, especially a very slow one, to hold the fly at this chosen level.

At one extreme, if you fish a Booby on a 30 cm leader behind a very fast sinking line which has been allowed to sink to the bottom,

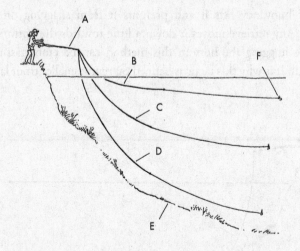

Fig. 28. Using various sinking lines to reach different depths.
A: Rod. B: Intermediate line. C: Slow-sinking line. D: Fast-sinking line.
E: Lake bed. F: Fly.

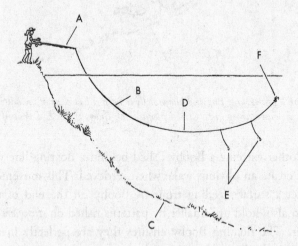

Fig. 29. Fishing a sinking line with a buoyant tail fly and droppers.
A: Rod. B: Sinking fly line. C: Lake bed. D: Leader.
E: Droppers and flies. F: Buoyant 'tail' fly.

115

the fly's buoyancy lifts it and prevents it from snagging on the bottom. Any retrieve moves it down a little towards the bottom. If trout are hugging the bottom this method can be embarrassingly successful. It is why this tactic is banned on many smaller trout lakes.

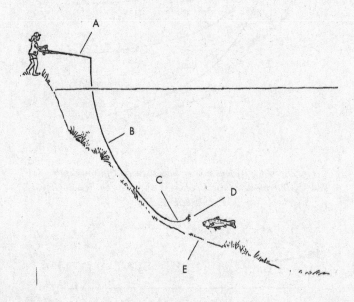

Fishing with a fast-sinking line and buoyant fly to keep it just clear of the bottom.
A: Rod. B: Fast-sinking line. C: Short leader. D: Buoyant fly. E: Lake bed.

At the other extreme a Booby fished behind a floating line will float and create an obvious wake when retrieved. This movement can attract a surface-feeding trout. A Booby on the end of the leader can also 'hold up' smaller fly patterns fished on *droppers* on the leader. The floating Booby ensures they are perfectly in the zone for trout feeding very close to the surface.

So while choice of fly pattern might be important, the depth at which you fish is more critical. If the trout are out of sight, keep experimenting to find the 'right' depth. If trout 'go off', think about changing the depth at which your flies are being fished before you resort to changing flies.

The techniques of fishing with sinking lines are pretty much the same if you are fishing from the bank or an anchored boat. The only difference is that the bank fisher may have to cope with a shelving shore and shallow water close to them which means their fly snags on the bottom if their line has sunk deeply. An anchored boat means you choose the depth of water below your feet which makes fly presentation easier. Fishing with sunk lines from a drifting boat on a big reservoir is more difficult because the boat is constantly moving. You cast downwind, but on windy days the boat is drifting quickly in the same direction. You have to retrieve fly line quickly just to keep in touch with your flies. There is not much time for sinking lines to sink! This is why most 'loch-style' fishers use a 'drogue', an underwater parachute, to slow down the speed of drift and have to use much faster sinking lines than they would use from the shore in an attempt to get down to their chosen depth.

The chapters that follow have much more on these tactics.

FOOD IS KEY

Why are the 'hot spots' at Elinor Trout Fishery consistently productive? What makes them different?

The first one is a small headland reaching out for 10 metres or so from a straight length of bank. The water is shallow at your feet but to the left it slopes steeply down into water that is 2 or 3 metres deep. To your right the water is shallower and in the summer weeds grow over this area. This means that straight in front of you the bottom slopes steeply. It acts like a trout magnet.

If you cast out to the left into the deeper water where the bottom is muddy you are covering an area that is attractive to *buzzers*, the insects described in Chapter 14. Buzzers need a muddy bottom for their larval homes and prefer a water depth of 2 to 3 metres.

If you cast to the right you are covering shallower water with more weeds and bottom cover. This area is much favoured by the *nymphs* of damselflies, a common freshwater insect, and by other abundant invertebrate prey such as freshwater *shrimps* which are all described in Chapter 13.

The sloping bottom straight ahead is a boundary between these two habitats and doubles your chances. As soon as your fly hits the water it may be taken by a trout patrolling the shallow water but if it continues to sink down the face of the slope it comes into sight of those trout that are feeding deeper down. Importantly, the steep slope acts as barrier, and therefore a turning point, for trout patrolling the deep water. These fish will be reluctant to change depth and are obliged to follow the face of the slope and thus stay in reach of your casts. On windy days underwater currents are created as the lake water is circulated by the waves. Features like underwater ridges and slopes magnify these currents and increase the trout prey they can carry. Trout are funnelled into these spots too.

Finally, the headland itself also tends to squeeze fish together even on calm days. Rainbow trout love to swim in loose shoals. If they are cruising along the line of a bank, some a few metres out from the shore, others far out from it, they become more concentrated off the end of a headland. Those that are long way out come into reach, while others that are close to the bank have to navigate round the headland.

A second hot-spot is at the end of a long, straight length of bank at the mouth of a bay. Straight in front of you the water is some of the deepest in the lake and it is within the reach of a long cast. Again, it is buzzer-rich territory. To your left the bottom slopes up gently into the shallow, weedy bay so you have the advantage of another, if more gentle, slope. However, what probably adds to the productivity of this spot is that the rounded, shallow bay acts like a receiving bowl for the wind and related currents that blow along the length of the lake. Any potential trout prey trapped on the surface ends up here. More importantly, if the wind blows into this bay for any time the surface currents created also concentrate the plankton-like *Daphnia,* or water flea, the trout's favourite food, there too. The trout follow.

The third Elinor hot-spot is different. It is also at the mouth of a shallow bay and the water which is in range all around you is only 1 or 2 metres deep. However, it is part of a channel because about 35 metres in front of you is a long, very shallow ridge which becomes very weedy in summer. If you wade out a little you can almost reach this ridge and fish close to the productive edge of the weeds. Takes do not only come there. The channel also seems to concentrate the trout. Perhaps they cruise into it and find they are in a cul-de-sac so they have to turn round to get back to the main body of the lake. You get two chances to show them your fly.

There is much more on tactics in Chapters 12 to 14.

Hot-spots do not always work. If you fish at any spot for half an hour and do not see trout rising, do not feel a *pull* nor see a trout swirl at your fly then you can be sure that the answer to the question, 'If I were a trout, where would I be today?' is 'Somewhere else.' That is where you should try too!

FISHING FROM A DRIFTING BOAT

Fishing from a drifting boat on a big water provides both an advantage and a disadvantage. The advantage is that you cover a lot of water and may find 'hot spots'. The disadvantage is that you quickly drift away from them. This is why there is so much skill in managing the drifting boat to increase the time spent in productive areas. For example, if the trout are finding fish in 2 or 3 metres of water, then a drift along a shoreline above that depth of water would be perfect. But, if the wind was blowing onto an area of that depth, the only way may be a series of short drifts from deep water towards the productive shore. This is why a ghillie or guide who knows the depths, the fishy areas and the best drifts in all wind directions is a valuable friend!

THE EXCEPTION TO THE RULE

None of these rules applies to upland, acid waters which are stocked with rainbow trout but offer them little natural feeding. Most trout in these waters are caught soon after they are stocked by fly fishers using lures fishing from well recognized, successful spots. These are often close to where the stocked trout were tipped into the water. They remain in shoals and tend to wander round together hugging the shore and staying close to their entry point for longer than the trout stocked in more productive waters which quickly spread out as they adapt to natural feeding.

Rainbow trout that find no food available seem to 'shut down'. You find their stomachs are empty and they can become very difficult to catch on any fly.

SUMMARY

WHERE ARE THE 'HOT SPOTS'?

- Windy conditions often stir up mud and discolour the water. Trout prefer clear water where they can see their prey if they can find it.
- Wind also creates underwater currents which funnel food and trout into bays and other features.
- In the early spring, before the weed growth becomes impenetrable, trout often search for food in the shallowest water.
- Large stones, rocky shores and weed beds provide cover for insect larvae, shrimps, etc. Trout will seek out these shorelines rather than those made up of gravel, small stones, sand or clay.
- From late March to early June the dominant food source will almost certainly be rising buzzer pupae. They emerge over muddy bottoms, often in 2 to 3 metres of water, and will often pull trout away from the shoreline to these productive areas.
- In most lakes, newly stocked trout follow the same dispersal pattern after they have been stocked. The regulars will know how they behave and where and how to catch them before they settle into natural feeding. Watch and learn!
- In late summer and autumn a lot of terrestrial flies are blown onto the water. Trout will be looking for them along the up-wind shore.

- If there are coarse fish their fry become vulnerable to predation by trout when the shallow water weed beds in which they have been hiding begin to die back in autumn. Many other insects and trout prey are similarly exposed. Fish above or close to dying weed beds.
- In hot weather trout can become distressed and will eventually stop feeding but before this they will head for the deepest, coolest water.

9
WHEN?

If you only go fishing when it is comfortable and convenient to you, you may not catch many trout.

WHAT TIME OF YEAR?

All trout and char, and their hybrid varieties, are cold water fish. They are 'fully operational' during a normal UK winter when water temperatures in still waters can get down to almost 0° Celsius and the ice may stop you fishing. At these temperatures the fish do not need the same amount of food to maintain their body weight as they do when the water warms up. They are less active but, in any case, there is less daylight available in which to feed.

Do not be put off trout fishing in the winter if you can stand the cold. The trout are not affected!

You may think there should be plenty of food available for trout in the winter months because of the large populations of prey, including insects like buzzers or damselfly nymphs that over-winter in ponds and lakes. But, in winter, these prey species are able to hide away. The buzzer larvae are tucked up in their mud tube homes and are not emerging to become adults. The damselfly larvae are living under stones and rotting water weeds and avoid swimming in open water.

To find such prey, trout cannot cruise about in mid-water waiting for it to appear. They have to search it out on the bottom, often nosing about among the stones and detritus, to flush out shrimps, the water hog louse *(Asellus sp.)*, nymphs and other tit-bits. To catch them a good bet is to use small, imitative flies and to get them down to the bottom. Fish them with a slow stop/start retrieve.

You may be surprised that high summer is not a great time for trout fishing except in upland, northern waters. In most of the UK the temperature of small still waters becomes too high for trout to be comfortable and they can effectively shut down. Fishery owners hope that temperatures do not rise so high that fatalities occur. Many responsible owners of small waters in southern England close their gates. There is no point in fishing for trout if water temperatures are much above 18° Celsius. You are unlikely to catch anything. Even if the temperature is low enough for trout to be feeding and active in high summer, some waters become heavily weeded or clouded by algae. Insect hatches become very sparse. It can be a very difficult time. You might want to take a summer holiday instead!

SPRINGTIME

Small water trout fisheries are busiest in the springtime. As water temperatures begin to rise in March the trout, like other cold-blooded creatures, need to eat more just to maintain their bodyweight and they become more active. Their need is rewarded by an explosion of insect activity in response to the lengthening days and the warming water.

The water is usually clear at this time of year because the excess of algae, which turns some waters pea green in the summer, will not become a problem until the temperature rises. As trout hunt by sight, clear water helps them. But, it also means they can examine your fly so, perhaps, is why they become choosy.

The first growth of microscopic plants can also trigger the first 'bloom' of the water flea *Daphnia*, a pin-head-sized crustacean, which trout love.

All this activity, and the increasing numbers of successful customers catching trout from commercial fisheries that have to be replaced, mean that more fish are stocked in spring than at any other time of year. *Stockies* are the easiest trout to catch.

If you are new to fly fishing, the spring is a good time to get started.

In early spring established (i.e. wild or not newly stocked) brown or rainbow trout become hungrier and they head for the shallow margins of lakes and ponds. This is where, in clear water, they will find a wide variety of prey species such as freshwater shrimps, water hog lice and a variety of insect nymphs and larvae. Trout are often seen nosing under, and dislodging, stones or weeds to get at the creepy crawlies underneath.

Newly stocked trout which are introduced at this time of year, or any time of year for that matter, also hug the bank in their new home where they often remain in loose shoals with the other trout stocked with them. You do not have to cast far to catch them!

THE IMPACT OF BUZZERS IN THE SPRING

The most prolific insect in all UK freshwaters is the *buzzer*. Although individual species vary, mostly the flying adults emerge between March and June.

Typically, buzzer pupae leave the protective mud in the morning and the trout will remain close to the bottom feeding on them as they emerge, often in immense concentrations. As the numbers emerging slow down, the trout follow the main mass of pupae up through the water. Often you have no clue what is happening until the trout become obvious when they start feeding within a foot of the surface. This happens as the 'hatch' is finally petering out!

You will learn much more about them and how to imitate them in Chapter 14.

OTHER INSECTS THAT EMERGE IN SPRING

A lot of other adult insects emerge from rivers and lakes as spring advances. In still waters, Pond Olives, one of the *Ephemeroptera sp.*

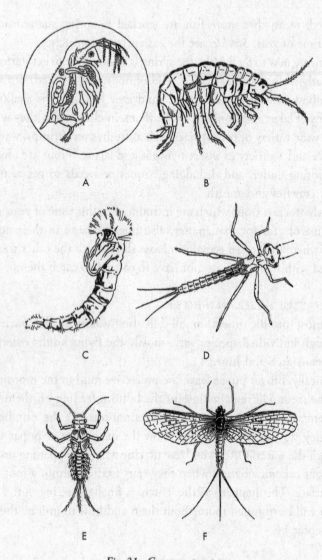

Fig. 31. Common trout prey.
A: Water flea (Daphnia) seen under a microscope. B: Shrimp (Gammarus) 8–
10mm. C: Buzzer pupa (Chironomus) 5–15mm.
D: Damselfly nymph 12–20mm. E: Pond olive nymph. F: Pond olive adult 10mm.

or 'up-wing' insect species, hatch in April and May. Trout take their fast swimming, dark brown nymphs with gusto. They emerge in shallow water and weed beds.

The further north you live the more variety of Ephemerid insects you will see hatching from large lakes and other still waters.

In the south of the UK or Ireland, and in a more limited number of northern areas, *Ephemeroptera danica,* the common Mayfly, is found in many lakes and streams. Trout gorge on their cream coloured nymphs as they emerge, from May to August, from the mud where they have lived over the winter. Often, trout selectively eat them at the surface as they struggle to make the transition from nymph to flying adult.

In June the first iridescent blue or green damselflies will appear. Their olive-green or brown nymphs often swim through open water to reach a plant stem or branch which they will use to crawl out of the water before hatching. Most still water trout have at least one or two damselfly nymphs in their stomachs during June and July, sometimes nothing else when they are abundant.

In summary, in the spring still waters are clear and their temperature is low enough to ensure that trout are eager to feed. There is plenty of natural feeding for them. Buzzers are king!

AUTUMN

As the nights lengthen, the water temperature drops, even if daytime temperatures are high. Trout fishing revives in small still waters.

Some spring-like buzzer hatches occur and some species will continue to emerge right through to Christmas on the milder days. Other freshwater insects such as water boatmen, damselfly nymphs, beetles and olive nymphs are at their maximum populations as the season's eggs have all hatched out. And, as the water weeds die off, all the creepy crawlies have less cover to hide in and become more available to hungry trout.

Terrestrial insects also have their last seasonal abundance before the winter and in some waters they become a significant food source for trout. The best example is the Crane Fly. They emerge in biggest numbers over pasture land. In some years they can be blown onto trout waters in huge numbers. They are helpless when they land on water and trout quickly learn which fields they are being blown off and where they will find them. An imitation 'Daddy' that is allowed to lie in the surface film where the breeze 'hits' the water and the ripple begins can be deadly!

If the water has a population of coarse fish the year's fry have grown into a substantial mouthful by autumn and they too become vulnerable as the weed beds die.

Trout continue to feed heavily if water temperatures remain above 10° Celsius.

Brown trout become sexually mature in preparation for their winter breeding season. They become more aggressive and gather at the mouth of any feeder streams.

In short, autumn is a good time to be a trout and a trout fisher. Do not miss out!

THE BEST TIME OF DAY TO FISH

Inevitably, many newly stocked trout do not enjoy their freedom from the stock ponds for long.

The smallest trout waters often stock every day if they have plenty of customers. Usually, they stock trout in the early morning before the anglers arrive. When the anglers are allowed onto the water there is sometimes an unseemly rush to be the first to show a fly to the naïve new trout.

WILD BROWN TROUT

It is not just naïve, newly stocked rainbow trout that are easier to catch in the morning. Experiments with wild brown trout show that they are most active in the first hours of daylight after being inactive, and presumably getting hungry, through the night. Having had this feeding spell they then become less active through the day before filling up again during another period of feeding in the evening right up to darkness. The fly fishers who pursue wild brown trout in wilderness areas like the highlands of Scotland and Wales have always known about this and remain, if they can, to enjoy the 'evening rise' on summer evenings.

Not quite as many get up before dawn.

RAINBOW TROUT

Rainbow trout seem to be more constant feeders through the day than brown trout. But, being the opportunists they are, both species ignore the rules if a 'fall' of terrestrial flies or a hatch of freshwater insects suddenly occurs. Overall, most experienced fly fishers do prefer the morning to the afternoon. This is worth thinking about if your time is limited.

Trout need daylight to be able to feed and therefore the short autumn days give them less time to fill up when the water temperature is still high and they have a high maintenance demand.

In the depths of winter, rainbow trout may not be quite as active as the temperature drops but they are soon enlivened by a spell of mild weather. Even if it is cold the sunlight will warm the water and the best chance is probably around mid-day.

INSECT EMERGENCE

Some insects emerge at predictable times. In the spring, buzzer pupae mostly rise to the surface during the morning so that lots of adults are seen to be hatching, and fish rising to them, around the middle of the day. By mid-afternoon it is all over. As summer arrives, buzzer hatches get later and some species leave the water at dusk. Beware, these rises do not happen every night, so do not depend on an evening rise. On some fine summer evenings nothing happens!

The best advice is to observe your local water carefully and to keep a record. All waters are different but the same pattern is usually repeated year on year.

SUMMARY

WHAT TIME OF YEAR?
- Any time except high summer and high water temperatures.
- Springtime is easiest.

WHAT TIME OF DAY?
- Start early in the morning if you can.
- Surface feeding on hatching buzzer pupae means the trout were feeding on them 2 metres down a few hours ago!
- Brown trout mostly feed early morning and in the evening.
- In winter/early spring concentrate on the middle of the day; for the rest of the year mornings are best.

10
HOW?
USING LURES AND ATTRACTORS

Those fly fishers who are experts in the use of lures are usually happy to give away examples of their favourite flies, to explain what lines they use and to go into great detail about the set-ups and retrieves that work for them. When beginners try to copy them, even fishing right beside them, it does not always work. There is more to fishing successfully with lures than a few flies and a single technique.

These experts have something extra which is best described as 'good hands'. They possess a combination of three attributes that are easier to explain than to replicate.

The first is an unerring ability to be 'in touch' with their flies at all times. This is a combination of the technical skills of casting and retrieving, alongside an instinctive ability to feel, or see, the most tentative interest of an inquisitive trout and, vitally, to react correctly.

The second is concentration. It is easy to concentrate when you expect a take at any second, but it is a different matter if you have been fishing for hours to no avail. It is easy to let your mind wander so that when the take finally comes, it does little more than wake you out of a day dream! The experts are not distracted from the job in hand. They have an uncanny ability to convert an interested trout into a well-hooked one.

The third is application. Most experts practise a lot. They know what to do because they were fishing yesterday, and the day before, and last week. They can answer the 'where?', 'when?' and 'how?' questions with certainty.

All this adds up to a confidence that they are doing the right thing and that success will come. It is a unique combination of practised, technical skill and an insight into what makes trout tick.

Pray that you too can acquire 'good hands'.

Fifty years ago most still water trout fishing took place in the northern and Celtic fringes of the UK. Their quarry was wild brown trout and sea trout. The local fly fishers made use of a huge number of *traditional* flies. They were *dressed* using the furs and feathers from the birds and animals they were familiar with or tinsels which came from the shelves of the local milliner. Most flies were dressed on small hooks (size 10 or 12) and they all had the same insect-based outline. Despite their *wings*, usually made of feather fibre, positioned over the *body* of the fly, these flies were *wet* flies. They were designed to fish just below the surface of the lakes or lochs where they were used.

If you talked to these fly fishers about what their flies copied or represented, many of them would have struggled to explain. Most had limited knowledge of entomology and they would have suggested that some of their dull-coloured flies did imitate common insects which, perhaps, had been 'drowned' while hatching. But, even in those distant days, when the fly fisher's quarry was always wild brown trout, experts knew that they needed two categories of flies. Some were clearly 'imitative' and were assumed to be taken by the trout feeding on the natural fly. Others, however, were unashamed *attractors*. They were the same shape and size but dressed with bright, unnatural materials. They were labelled as *fancy* flies. And, they worked! Millions of words were written extolling the virtues of different fly patterns and where and when they would succeed. These flies work just as well today. Many traditional flies, both imitative and fancy are still used throughout the world.

If you fish upland lakes and lochs today for wild brown trout, and the rainbow trout now stocked in some of them, you would be unwise not to arm yourself with traditional flies such as Black Pennell, Soldier Palmer, Mallard and Claret, and Silver Invicta. Some hardened old hands would say these are the only patterns you need, but as there are many hundreds of traditional flies to choose from why be so cynical? Which of these are imitative flies, which are attractors or fancies? In truth, no one is absolutely sure!

Fancy flies are definitely the predecessors of today's lures. They are now mostly made of synthetic, riotously coloured and fluorescent materials. No longer do they copy the shape or size of traditional flies and they certainly make no pretence of mimicking any living thing.

MODERN LURES

Today you will not find many traditional flies in the fly boxes of the modern still water fly fishers who fish for rainbow trout in the lakes and reservoirs of lowland England. Instead their box will be full of more wildly coloured flies, often bigger than size 10. They will label them 'lures'.

You should be clear about two facts.

Firstly, the majority of the trout caught from southern reservoirs and all other commercial still waters are caught on lures, not on imitative flies. This is not the impression you get from the angling literature which, perhaps inevitably, leans to a more romantic view of trout sipping down perfect imitations of their favourite insects.

Secondly, newly stocked rainbow trout, often referred to as *stockies* by fly fishers, are very vulnerable to brightly coloured lures and many succumb to their charms very soon after they are put into their new home.

LURES AND STOCKIES

It is easy to get a bit snooty about catching 'easy', new stockies on lures. This temptation should be avoided. Anglers get what they demand and pay for from fishery owners. It is better to be able to fly fish for 'easy', top quality trout than to have no fishing at all. And, if you are just getting started at trout fly fishing it is great to catch some fish and not to worry too much about their pedigree. Remember, you do not have to target 'easy' new fish if you do not want to. Newly stocked trout tend to hang about in a shoal near their point of release, sometimes for a few hours, sometimes for a few days. If you are catching trout after trout and when you *spoon* them you find that their stomachs are still full of the trout pellets they had for breakfast you can always move and fish somewhere else on the lake.

It is also not obligatory to fish in small, heavily stocked waters. Most fly fishers get started there but rapidly develop wider horizons. There is no shortage of opportunities to target 'difficult' fish in different and challenging waters.

WHY DO TROUT TAKE LURES?

No one can tell you why trout take lures, but plenty of your fellow fishers will try.

It is wiser to concentrate on 'what works' and to develop your own approach, driven by what works for you. There are no rules here. No one, no matter what they may say, really understands why a fish takes one lure but not another. This is why fly dressers constantly create new lures which often become ridiculously fashionable for a short time. Enjoy experimenting but base your personal strategy on the guidance below and the fundamentals of fly fishing with lures.

Trout respond to the stimuli of lures and attractors differently from the way they attack natural food items. They respond like a kitten that cannot resist reacting to a moving plaything. The kitten 'practises' pouncing on, and intercepting it, and can be encouraged to more active 'play' by exaggerated or unexpected movements.

In clear water you will see similar trout behaviour. Sometimes several trout will be attracted by a lure and will track it as it moves through the water. Some will 'nip' at its tail but not swallow it. The eventual 'take' is usually the result of a sudden change in the way it moves... perhaps because the lure stops, suddenly accelerates or changes depth.

If you cannot see the fish all this has to be imagined. You must *work* the lure to entice the trout to finally snaffle it!

HOW TO USE LURES AND ATTRACTORS

When you are getting started at fly fishing, floating lines are the easiest to cast and are recommended. The floating line helps you to see the speed at which you are retrieving a lure. Trout tend to follow a lure so the further you can cast, the better. The distance provides more time to entice a trout to finally pounce and take the lure properly.

The retrieve you choose is vital. Colour, size and shape of the lure can be important too, but how you make it behave is critical. Trout will take a lure when it is stationary, when it is falling through the water and at all speeds of retrieve. But, the most likely taking point is when the lure's movement, or lack of it, changes suddenly. Be ready. How you react is the key to whether you convert *takes* into *hook-ups*.

CHOOSE THE RIGHT DEPTH

When you cast out a lure on a floating line you need to let it sink unless you intend to retrieve it very close to the surface. If you have made a perfect cast the line will be lying in a straight line across the surface and you will be in direct contact with your lure. If the cast has not been perfect, retrieve the line as quickly as possible with your free hand to straighten the line. You need to be ready to feel any take.

Trout often take a slow sinking lure. Perhaps they are attracted by the splash as it hits the water. If you do feel a take, instantly clamp the line tightly with your index finger against the rod handle. The trout will hook itself against the tension of the tight line as long as the rod is pointing down the line. Wait until it feels well hooked before you lift the rod and start to play it. If it does not hook itself, do nothing. The trout will often return and take the lure again. It will not be able to find it if you have yanked the lure out of the water!

Decide how far you want your lure to sink. If you are fishing in a clear water fishery where you can see cruising trout they tell you the depth to aim for. In such a fishery estimating both the depth of the fish and the time it takes for your lure to get down to them can be tricky.

Trout are usually deeper than they appear. Even with heavily weighted lures it is easy to under estimate how long it takes the lure to get down. On small clear-water lakes individual, cruising trout can be stalked. A successful tactic is to cast the lure into the path of an approaching trout so that it sinks as close to its nose as possible, then the lure is twitched upwards to induce a response. This sounds easy but it is surprisingly tough to match the sinking rate of the fly and the approach of the trout.

Even if you are fishing at long range and in a lake where the trout are not so visible the same approach needs to be replicated. How deep do you think the trout are? How long will it take the lure to get there?

If you are not sure how deep they are, you have to experiment. Count your lure down to different depths before starting to retrieve. When you get a response, concentrate on that depth.

Expect a take the moment you start the retrieve. This first movement is often what induces a savage take. If you clamp tight, the trout will hook itself.

DO NOT REACT!

If there is no take 'on the drop' or as a result of the first movement you impart to the lure, what next?

When you retrieve lures you should expect to feel trout pecking and brushing the lure without getting hooked. These touches are often barely discernable or feel as if the lure has touched weed. Do not react. Keep retrieving. It is, without doubt, a continuing, uninterrupted retrieve that eventually triggers the solid take. It often comes towards the end of the retrieve when the lure changes direction.

Everything has to be tight if the fish is to hook itself. This means that the rod must be pointing straight down the line so that, as the trout takes, there is no flexing rod to cushion the contact. The fly line must be across your index finger so that it can instantly clamp the line tight in response to the take.

You will not hook them if you pull the lure away from the trout by striking and lifting the rod!

THE BEST RETRIEVE

There is no best retrieve for a lure but a 'long draw' retrieve, when the free hand pulls as much of a metre of line through the rod rings in a single, smooth movement, is usually better than jerky, short pulls.

It also helps to vary the speed of the retrieve. There are no hard-and-fast rules. Sometimes a slow deliberate retrieve is best, especially if the water is cold. But, by contrast, when trout are feeding heavily on coarse fish fry in the summer and autumn, the fastest possible retrieve with the lure creating a 'V' in the surface film is often what works.

THE ROLY-POLY RETRIEVE

Recently, many fly fishers have taken this tactic one step further. They are convinced that a smooth, uninterrupted retrieve, no matter what speed they choose, is best. They use the 'roly-poly' retrieve. They hold the rod butt between their elbow and their body and use both hands, one after the other, to continuously retrieve the line. This cuts out the pause that inevitably results when your free hand has to re-grasp the line when doing a conventional retrieve. The roly-poly retrieve has the valuable additional advantage of preventing you, as you have not got hold of it, from striking with the rod when you get a take. Simply continuing the retrieve hooks the trout firmly.

There are other tricks to try!

If you are getting taps from trout that are not developing into hard, solid takes try suddenly stopping the retrieve. Sometimes the trout will take properly when the lure stops, but it is more likely to take hard when it suddenly starts moving again.

Alternatively, try speeding up the retrieve in response to taps and pecks.

Finally, at the end of the retrieve, do not rush to re-cast. Let the lure sink naturally for a few seconds, or to 'hang', in the water at your feet. This is a particularly important tactic if you are fishing from an anchored or drifting boat, especially when fishing with a sunk line. Sometimes a long 'hang' of up to a minute is successful. It is vital to watch the line and to react to any movement at all, as following trout sometimes 'mouth' the lure without swimming off with it. Experts mark their lines so that they know when to lift their rod tips to execute a perfect 'hang'. Trout often rush in to grab a lure they have been following as it gets into shallower water or when it stops. As you have lifted your rod in preparation for your next cast and to 'hang' the lure, when the trout finally takes it you will need to strike hard to hook it because there is no longer a straight, tight line between your hand and the fish. Try not to lift the rod tip so high that you cannot strike if necessary.

THE COLOURS OF LURES

There are no limitations to the colours, sizes or shapes of trout lures.

No one knows 'why' a trout takes a lure. Perhaps there is a magic colour combination waiting to be discovered that will prove to be irresistible to every trout all the time. No one has found it yet.

Current experience gives a few pointers to what makes a good lure and some popular examples are described below. Some fly fishers would say these are all the lures you need. They are certainly three excellent, well-proven, highly adaptable patterns.

	Orange	White	Black
Hook Size	10		
Tying Thread	Orange	White	Black
Tail	Orange marabou	White marabou	Black marabou
Rib	None	Silver wire	None
Tag	None		Fluorescent green chenille
Body	Fluorescent 'Fritz' Chenille to match the tail		
Wing	None		
Hackle	None		
Head	None	Fluorescent green chenille	None

These are in the most popular and essential colours of lures. Their names are the Orange Tadpole, the Cat's Whisker, and the Black and Green Tadpole. They are must-have lures.

A variation is tying them on bigger or smaller hooks. Small lures often work when more 'normal' sizes fail. They can be 'bulked up' by adding a wing of similar coloured marabou. This often works if the water is cloudy and visibility is poor.

These lures can be weighted by adding gold or silver beads as additional 'heads'.

If you remove all or most of the marabou tails from these lures they become *Blobs*. These flies were invented when their length had

Fig. 32. Lures.
Top: Orange Tadpole.
Middle: Cat's Whisker (white tail, green body).
Bottom: Black and Green Tadpole.

to be reduced to comply with competition rules restricting the length of flies. Many believe that, by happy accident, this improved their effectiveness and hooking ability.

Add a pair of similar coloured *plastazote* balls to the heads of these lures and they become 'Boobies'. These are essential lures when buoyancy is required.

These variations to the three lures described above are just the start. Lures can be dressed in a huge number of other colours and combinations. Some fly fishers swear by pink and 'sunburst yellow' lures. They all work at times but orange, white and black remain firm favourites. Remember, the depth they are fished at is probably more important than their colour.

Hopefully, this is encouraging you to learn to tie lures and other flies for yourself as part of getting started to trout fish. There are, of course, lots of lures available in fishing tackle shops but it is fun to experiment. If you 'roll-your-own' you are able to create unique flies and lures that look exactly how you want them to. If you are tempted, do not forget the basic advice below.

THE ESSENTIAL VARIATIONS

WEIGHTED LURES

If you fish with lures using a floating line, their sinking speed depends on the weight of the lure. Heavier lures made by using lead wire under the body, or with gold or silver beads as heads, get the fly down quicker. Some small lures used in clear water fisheries where trout are targeted for 'sight' fishing consist of nothing more than twists of lead wire and a few turns of seal fur. These are known as *bugs* but are simply specialized lures designed to sink quickly into the path of a cruising trout where it is tweaked upwards to tempt an induced take.

BEAD HEADS

Well known lures are often enhanced by the addition of a gold or silver bead, placed just behind the eye of the hook. Of course, these patterns sink more quickly than the standard dressings so you do not have to wait so long before starting to retrieve.

They have other potential advantages. A bead-weighted fly sinks through the water more quickly than the standard pattern. This exaggerated movement may be more attractive to a trout. Similarly, trout seem to find lures that change depth when the retrieve stops more attractive than those that stay at the same depth. The extra weight of a bead headed lure means that whenever the retrieve stops, the lure instantly starts to dive down until the retrieve starts again. This 'rise-and-fall' retrieve is a vital trigger to some trout.

SINKING LINES

When a lure is fished on a floating line and it has been allowed to sink, the first retrieve will pull the lure upwards towards the surface. This may be an attractive enticement that induces some trout to take but if it does not, and the retrieve is continued, then even weighted lures will soon be being retrieved not far below the surface.

This is no good if the fish are well down in the water. Trout are always reluctant to change depth. Deep lying fish are simply not vulnerable to the charms of the lure high above their head.

But, fishing the same lure on a sinking line that is allowed to sink after casting to the required depth, permits a level retrieve to be made. The lure remains at the 'right' depth throughout most of the retrieve. This type of retrieve is always more successful for deep lying trout than using a lure fished behind a floating line. Even if the trout prefer the rise-and-fall of a weighted lure it is best if it is moving along at the right level.

There is a range of sinking lines designed to sink at different rates. Sinking lines that are labelled 'DI 3, DI 5 and DI 7' mean they sink at 3, 5 and 7 inches per second respectively. Fly fishers who search for trout in big, deep lakes need to own several different sinking lines to fish effectively for trout lying at different depths and they can spend their whole day experimenting to find the right one.

In smaller, shallower waters, especially if you are fishing from the bank and not from a boat, all that you need is an 'intermediate' line which sinks slowly. You may need a bit of patience before starting a retrieve while you wait for it to sink, but it will bring the lure back at your chosen depth.

If you will be fishing with lures regularly from a boat or in deep water, a range of sinking lines is an essential purchase.

Sinking lines are more difficult to cast. The line must be on the surface, and straight out in front, before an overhead cast can be made. You will need an initial roll cast to get a sinking line onto the surface at the end of each retrieve.

Do not attempt to overhead cast a line which is sunk below the surface! You will break your rod.

FLOATING LURES

The most popular lures used for trout today are Boobies. These lures are tied with a pair of *plastazote* balls just behind the hook eye. This highly buoyant material means they float. Their buoyancy can be reduced by trimming the size of the balls.

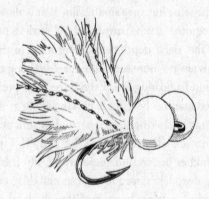

Fig. 33. Buoyant 'Booby' lure.

Why are they so useful and so successful?

One reason is often forgotten. Although trout hunt by sight, they are very sensitive to vibration and a fly with a buoyant, or a bead head, will give off significant vibrations as it is pulled through the water. If the Booby is fished using a floating line, its buoyancy will keep it right on the surface. Any retrieve will create lots of vibration and a wake. This disturbance can be irresistible to trout, particularly those hunting coarse fish fry in the summer or autumn.

If a Booby is fished using a sinking line, it will eventually be pulled below the surface as the line goes down. Retrieving the line mirrors the effect of a weighted fly behind a floating line. Every stop in the retrieve allows the buoyant fly to drift upwards producing a rise-and-fall retrieve. This can be carried out at a much slower speed than is possible with a weighted fly. There are times when trout only seem to want lures retrieved very slowly. The sunk line/floating lure combination also keeps the lure deep but above a weedy or snag littered bottom.

There is one tactic that makes Boobies indispensable. Trout, especially when the water is either very cold or too hot, seek out the deepest water in the lake and can shoal there in large numbers. They will ignore any fly or lure that does not get right down to their depth. A deadly tactic is to cast a Booby into this deep water, usually using a fast sinking line. The Booby is attached to the end of the fly line on the shortest of leaders, usually only 30 cm or so, and the lure is taken right down to the bottom as the sinking line settles there. Its buoyancy keeps the Booby just off the bottom. Often there is no need to move the lure to induce a take, but any short, sharp retrieve will cause the Booby to dart towards the bottom. 'Slam' takes are the result. This tactic can be so successful that it is banned by some fishery owners.

There is one final trick using Boobies that is probably not lure fishing at all but is invaluable. The counteracting effect of a slow sinking/intermediate fly line and a carefully trimmed buoyant Booby on a long leader can make the lure 'hover' at a desired depth. It is not only lures that are attractive to trout when fished in this way. Flies that imitate insect nymphs or buzzer pupae on short droppers tied at metre gaps further up the leader can be very effective too when 'held' at the right depth. This tactic is known as the 'washing line method'. It is usually described as a way to fish imitative flies but trout are just as likely to take the lure as they are to be fooled by the imitations. A variation of this tactic, using a floating line, is to employ two Boobies, one on the end of the leader (the tail fly) and one as the first dropper nearest to the fly line so that you can fish one or two imitative flies on short droppers in between them. This trick ensures the imitative flies remain very close to the surface. An essential tactic if the trout are selectively feeding right at the surface and ignoring flies or lures deeper down.

A warning! It is not easy to cast out two Boobies on a leader with one or two droppers. Your casting technique has to be perfect to prevent horrendous tangles. It pays not to be over-ambitious if you are just getting started. If you think this tactic is essential use just one dropper until you are confident about the quality of your casting.

DAPHNIA FEEDERS

The food of choice for all loch and lake trout, brown or rainbow, whether they are 'wild' or newly stocked, is the tiny crustacean, *Daphnia*.

The common name for *Daphnia* is the water flea. Each individual is about the size of a pin head. They have a remarkable similarity to a flea we might find on our dog or cat but these tiny crustaceans are not parasites. They feed on microscopic plants and algae in the water and they can be present in enormous numbers or 'blooms' when conditions are right for them. Like all crustaceans they have hard shells and the water needs to be calcium rich. They exist in those productive, lowland lakes which also support other animals that need calcium to build shells such as freshwater shrimps and snails. They are all 'indicator' species for *Eutrophic* or fertile, freshwater habitats.

Although *Daphnia* can swim, they live in open water and are subject to the wind currents that build up in lakes. If the wind blows in one direction for days the *Daphnia* bloom will end up down wind and the trout will follow them. *Daphnia* seem to prefer a certain light intensity, probably related to the algae they feed on so they swim down when the light is bright during sunny days but swim towards the surface if it is dull or as darkness approaches. The trout follow. This is another reason there is often an evening rise of trout.

Although there can be *Daphnia* blooms early in the year when the lake water first begins to warm in March and April they are more typical later in the year when lakes become a little 'greener' as algae and microscopic plants flourish.

The relationship between *Daphnia* and trout is similar to the dependence of the giant baleen whales of the Southern Ocean on the small, shrimp-like crustaceans, or *Krill*, on which they feed. Both whales and trout can cruise through these high protein, solid shoals of tiny creatures with their mouths open and make an easy living. It is food to wax fat on!

Grafham Water in Cambridgeshire is famous for its fast growing, *Daphnia*-feeding trout. These trout, during years of heavy blooms, eat little else throughout the late spring and summer. A rainbow trout stocked at 2 lb in March can weigh 4 lb by October. It tastes wonderful.

When you spoon a *Daphnia*-feeding trout you usually find it is their sole diet. It looks like green sludge but if you dip your spoon into the water you will see all the tiny water fleas. It is hardly surprising trout do not bother to waste energy chasing other prey when *Daphnia* are available to them. This is frustrating for the traditional fly fisher armed with insect imitating flies. No one has yet invented a fly to imitate an individual, pin-head-sized water flea!

There is an answer. For many years fly fishers have known that some lures can grab a trout's attention for long enough to divert them from *Daphnia* and persuade them to chase and take it. It is not always easy. The *Daphnia*-feeding trout is not hungry. They often swirl at, or chase, a lure but it may be hard to convert this interest into a firm take. Brightly coloured lures are best and orange has always been a good bet.

Brightly coloured traditional flies like the Dunkeld or Kingfisher Butcher have also worked on *Daphnia*-feeding trout for a hundred years. More recent inventions like the *Orange Blob,* which is nothing more than eye-burning, fluorescent, orange, Fritz Chenille wrapped round a hook shank, is top-of-the-pops today.

It is vital to ensure that lures fishing for *Daphnia*-feeding trout are fished at the right depth. These trout are feeding at a depth dictated by the *Daphnia* and are reluctant to move from it. To have the best chance any lure should be fished for as long as possible at this depth while it is being retrieved. You will inevitably need a sinking line, such as an intermediate, and you will need to experiment to find the right depth. And, do not forget, if takes dry up it is probably not because the lure pattern is wrong, it is more likely that the 'right' depth has changed in response to the light level.

A FAST RETRIEVE

Perhaps because they are called 'lures' many fly fishers believe they need to be retrieved quickly. This is not true. The skill of lure fishing is to discover the right speed, or the variation in speed of retrieve, that works on the day. But, there are times when a very fast retrieve should be tried.

If trout are hunting coarse fish fry, which are abundant in some trout lakes in the summer and autumn, they seem to have two means of attack. The most dramatic is when a loose shoal of trout 'pen' a large number of fry against a solid feature from which they cannot escape, perhaps a dying weed bed, a pier or other structure which, because of the protection it normally affords, is sought out by fry. The trout crash into the shoal of fry, often with dramatic splashes, and then sweep round to mop up any stunned fry that are not able to swim away. The best way to catch these trout is to cast a floating fry imitation, perhaps one with 'Booby' eyes into the scene of carnage, leave it still, and hope that a returning trout wallops it.

The second approach by fry-feeding trout is to cruise slowly round an ambush area where they expect fry to be. These are the trout that seem to be particularly vulnerable to a fast moving lure, especially a white one. The faster you can make it move the better. If it slows down they often turn away. This tactic often works best when there is a strong wind and big waves on the water. This seems to excite the trout, especially in the summer months of August and early September, perhaps because the fry have become disorientated by the waves.

An additional trick worth trying is to use a white buoyant lure, 'Booby' eyes again perhaps, and to race it through the waves so that it creates plenty of wake in its path. The *smash* takes that can result are as exciting as fly fishing gets.

It is often difficult to convert interest ('they keep following my lure!') from *Daphnia-* and fry-feeding fish into firm takes. Try speeding up the retrieve. It is impossible to know what will switch such fish 'on' but a high speed chase sometimes does. Do not forget to suddenly stop the retrieve and to let the lure just sink under its own weight for a few seconds before you lift it from the water at the end of the retrieve. This change of speed often triggers a solid take too.

A SLOW RETRIEVE

Just as there are times when a fast variation of the standard 'long draw' retrieve of your lure works better, there are also times when the slowest of retrieves can pay dividends. This is particularly true in winter and spring when the water temperature is below 10° Celsius and the trout are not as active as they will be later in the season.

It can be deadly to anchor a Booby to the bottom using a fast sinking line and a very short leader. While this technique is most often used to target deep lying trout who have sought the coolest part of a lake or pond in hot weather, it also works in shallower water at other times of the season. Trout will take the Booby when it is stationary and some anglers do little more than cast out and ensure the fly line remains tight as they wait to feel a take. Takes are usually savage and the trout hook themselves as long as the line is held tightly as they swim off against it.

In the colder months of the year trout tend to favour shallow water, often where weeds will grow later in the year or where the bottom is covered in large stones, because this is where insect larvae and free swimming nymphs are seeking sanctuary. Trout hunting around these 'features' will ignore flies and lures being fished quickly over their heads. A better bet is a lure fished slowly and close to the bottom. Remember the kitten chasing a ball of wool! It is movement that alerts and interests it. A slow 'stop-and-start' retrieve can keep a trout following for metres before it finally grabs the lure firmly. You can use a buoyant Booby but other lures will work just as well as long as you are not constantly hooking snags. If you make sure a lure fished using a floating line is right on the bottom before starting to retrieve, the lift provided by the floating line may induce a take. If not, let the lure drop to the bottom again and repeat some slow stops-and-starts. There is no limitation to variations of movement you can try. Remember the first rule of fly fishing – 'If what you are doing is not working, do something else!'

THE CRITICAL MOMENT...!

No matter what speed you are retrieving a lure, there is one time above all when you should expect a take. This is the moment when a lure, after being retrieved for some time, suddenly changes depth. This is normally towards the end of the retrieve, especially when using a sinking or intermediate fly line, and you are getting ready to re-cast and are lifting the rod. Presumably, a following trout does not want to change depth. They have to grab the lure or lose it.

SUMMARY

RETRIEVING LURES

- Newly stocked rainbow trout are inquisitive, use bright colours.
- Expect takes 'on-the-drop'.
- Experiment to find the 'right' depth.
- Ignore taps and pecks, keep retrieving until you get a hard, solid take.
- Always point the rod down the line, clamp the line with your finger to hook the fish before lifting the rod.
- Experiment to find the best speed of retrieve, try long draws first.
- If the retrieve you are using is not working, do something else!

MAKING LURES WORK

- Black is a good colour when the water is cold in the winter and early spring.
- A touch of fluorescent green seems to enhance the attraction of lures.
- White lures are attractive to trout feeding on coarse fish fry.
- Orange lures work at all times of year and are the best bet for *Daphnia*-feeding trout.
- Marabou feather fibres provide lots of movement in lures.
- Modern synthetic materials that provide flash and reflect light provide valuable additional attraction to, or are replacing, traditional fur and feathers.
- Lures do not need to be big! Try them tied on size 10 or smaller hooks.

EXTRA ATTRACTION
- Use weighted bead head lures to get deeper and create a 'sink-and-draw' action.
- Use buoyant Boobies, a short leader and a fast sinking line to retrieve close to the lake bed.
- Sinking lines ensure a level retrieve at the chosen depth.
- Try a fast retrieve on hot, windy days.

AND FINALLY
- If all else fails, use an intermediate line and a black lure and search different depths... it often works when you are desperate!

11

HOW?
USING IMITATIVE FLIES
HELPFUL BASIC BIOLOGY

No one knows why a trout chases and takes a brightly coloured lure that looks nothing like any prey species it has ever eaten.

But, use a little skill, observe a feeding trout and cast your artificial fly, a few wisps of feather or fur, close to it and you will see it confidently taken as it is mistaken for another passing tit-bit. Fooling a feeding trout to take a fly that imitates its prey is the very essence of fly fishing.

Libraries of fishing books tell the novice how complicated it is to identify the hundreds of prey species that trout feed on. They offer thousands of fly patterns to try. They explain how frustrating it can be to fool any trout at times, even when they are evidently feeding hard. The purpose of the next few chapters is to provide some directions through this maze.

Getting started in this way will not provide simple answers to complex problems. It should teach you to see what is not obvious and to understand the trout's world. It is the start of an enjoyable journey.

You do not need to be a freshwater biologist to be a fly fisher but it helps! There is some basic science every fly fisher needs to know.

PRODUCTIVITY
The biology of any lake or pond depends on the source of the water that creates it. Almost all lakes and ponds in the lowlands of the UK have a water source that contains adequate calcium and other dissolved minerals to support abundant life. Scientists label such lakes *Eutrophic* or 'fertile'. These are 'productive' lakes. They

support the greatest variety and, more importantly, the greatest numbers of invertebrates, including freshwater shrimps, mussels and snails that need calcium to build their shells. In these waters all fish, including trout, can find plenty to eat especially in the warmer months of the year.

In mountainous, more barren areas of the UK and Ireland, such as the Scottish Highlands, many lakes and lochs of all sizes have more acidic water sources and they lack dissolved minerals and nutrients. These waters are *Oligotrophic* or 'infertile'. They are easy to identify. Lift a large stone out of the water. On its underside you will probably see small, active insect larvae that fly fishers call 'nymphs'. But, there will be no snails or shrimps, the calcium-dependant 'indicator' species, which would always be present in a *Eutrophic* lake.

Some *Oligotrophic* lakes and lochs are so infertile that they can hardly support life, including trout, but these are very rare. However, if you are visiting a mountainous or upland area to fish, it is important to choose a lake that has a good reputation and a healthy population of wild trout. Many do not!

The wild trout in infertile waters inevitably struggle to find enough to eat and are often very small. Large rainbow trout are sometimes stocked in such waters and they struggle to survive too. In the most infertile, stocked rainbows can find nothing to eat. After their initial, inquisitive interest in lures they switch off completely and become almost impossible to catch. They slowly starve to death and never survive a winter.

Fortunately, many *Oligotrophic* waters do support healthy populations of aquatic insects adapted to these conditions, particularly stoneflies, sedges and some *Ephemeroptera* or 'olives'. The 'nymphs' of all these insects emerge from their hiding places to become flying adults in the spring and summer. These hatches provide welcome seasonal feasts for resident trout, whether wild or stocked.

These trout also depend hugely on terrestrial insects blown onto the water. Fortunately, in the warm months, the wild countryside around these upland lakes and lochs is insect rich.

Some *Eutrophic* waters are found in surprising places. In the far north west of Scotland, surrounded by peat bogs and heather, there are clear, weedy fertile lochs that lie over isolated limestone bed rock. There are similar lochs on the Orkney Islands and others close to the shores of some of the isles of the Outer Hebrides. These waters, like the famous limestone lakes of Ireland, are all capable of supporting big populations of fast growing, wild brown trout if they are properly managed.

Common sense trout fly fishing lore results from this science.

WATER DEPTH AND LOCATION

In the infertile waters there are no *Daphnia* or any other plankton-like animals in open water. Trout find nearly all their potential prey in shallow water and this is where they will be. The wise, traditional advice from Scottish boatmen and ghillies is, 'If ye canna see the bottom, you're fishing water that's tae deep.' It is advice worth heeding!

It is also vital to choose shore lines and shallows that are covered with rocks and stones. The stonefly and olive nymphs, which are the commonest food of trout in these lakes, cling to large rocks and stones. They do not live on sandy or gravel bottoms or on cliff like shores where they cannot get shelter under stones or other protective features. Thus, although many of these wild waters are large, the productive areas for fishing can be remarkably small. These 'hot' areas also change as different insect species hatch or as the wind direction alters. Wild brown trout are also territorial and protect their feeding areas.

In short, you need to keep moving to be successful on these wild waters.

THE WEATHER

The weather affects insect activity and hatches almost as much as the calendar. Emerging insects need, and wait for, high humidity before appearing. Fly fishers pray for damp southerly or westerly breezes. They are glum during periods of high pressure that mean lots of sunshine and dry winds.

Even in fertile waters where trout are not so dependent on insect prey, dry sunny days, especially if it is also windy, are often the kiss of death. On such days it pays to concentrate on early mornings and late evenings.

In cold weather there are days when the water looks leaden and just as dead. Later in the year there are hot, brassy days when the dry wind seems to have exterminated all living things. On such days wild brown trout become moribund, especially in infertile waters. They need to be 'woken' by a hatch or a *fall* of terrestrial insects. Even in fertile waters, where there are many more shrimps, snails and other prey available, trout can be hard to come by when there is no insect activity. How should you respond to such difficult conditions?

On wild trout waters most fly fishers stick with traditional flies, perhaps using an intermediate line to fish them a bit deeper. One option is to fish with lures. Another is to use one of the many imitative flies that fly fishers call 'nymphs'. They mimic the size, shape and colour of fresh water insects. These flies have a tail, a body, a thorax and head like the real thing. They have no wings just like the natural nymph. The obvious advantage of imitative flies is that they will interest trout that have learnt to ignore lures.

Artificial nymphs do not work miracles. They still have to be fished at the right depth and in the right place to attract a trout. Even in the worse conditions there will still be some vulnerable trout that are 'grazing' around prey-rich features anticipating the next emergence of buzzers or other insects.

Nymphs are not a desperation tactic. The imitative nymph, fished well down, when there is no insect activity, can be exactly the same fly you would use close to the surface when insects are emerging.

Happily, there are also perfect fly fishing days when the lakeside air hums with emerging insects and the water is dimpled by vulnerable, rising trout. If only there were more of them!

DO NOT BELIEVE EVERYTHING YOU SEE

You need practice, inquisitiveness and objectivity to interpret what you see.

For example, it is easy to see large numbers of insects on the wing and plenty of rising trout and assume you can see what the trout are feeding on. But, perhaps the insects you see flying about hatched yesterday and the trout are feeding on something different. Only the contents of a trout's stomach give a clear picture of its diet today.

Remember that the weather and conditions, not the time it is convenient for us to fish, dictate the natural cycles. And, we have terrible memories. Keep a written record. When you fish your favourite water make a brief note of the date, the conditions, what you saw, what the trout were eating and how they were caught. Nothing improves your expertise year on year more than this accumulated knowledge.

Treasure it!

SUMMARY

- Trout behaviour is dictated by the 'productivity' of their environment.
- In *oligotrophic* waters trout inhabit the shallows; in *eutrophic* waters they are found in open water and at a range of depths because a greater range of prey is available.
- Weather controls insect behaviour; trout respond accordingly.
- Learn to match what you see around you to what you find in the stomach of the trout you catch.
- Keep a record. What happened last year will happen again this year.

12

HOW?
USING IMITATIVE FLIES
THE THREE BEST NYMPHS

Hundreds of species of freshwater insects, snails, crustaceans and fish share their habitat with trout. Almost all of them have, at some time, been found in the stomach of a trout. Brown and rainbow trout are opportunistic predators with the most catholic of tastes. Later chapters concentrate on the prey species that trout eat most. They do not proscribe 'if they are eating this, you do that' advice. Instead you are encouraged to observe and to understand what makes feeding trout vulnerable to imitative flies and how to fish them.

It is a myth that an exact imitation of a trout's prey is the best fly. This chapter describes three 'must-have' flies that will catch trout anywhere in the world. These flies are 'imitative' in size, shape and colour but they are not imitations of a specific prey. What does a trout see in them? Who cares? They work!

Does that mean no other imitative flies are necessary? Of course not! They do not always work. You would be a fly fisher who has no soul if you do not celebrate the truth that sometimes only one fly will do and that a great joy of fly fishing is to 'match-the-hatch'.

The message is that there is more to fly fishing than finding an imitative fly. It is what you do with it that counts.

THE BEST NYMPHS IN THE WORLD

The three nymph patterns listed below, or flies very like them, would be recognized anywhere in the world where fly fishers chase trout. If you are persistent but still cannot fool a trout with one of these on the end of your leader you have hit an unusual day.

They are the *Gold Ribbed Hare's Ear* (usually GRHE), the *Cruncher* and a *Red Diawl Bach*. No one knows why these 'generalist' nymphs (as opposed to exact imitations of natural insects) work so well. Their effectiveness is a distillation of a hundred years of continuing experimentation by fly fishers. You will need to experiment too to find the correct retrieve for them on the day.

The purpose of this chapter is to assure you that you are able to catch trout on imitative flies even if you are confused by the complex biology of the place you fish and the behaviour of the trout that live there. Use these three flies! Hopefully, this will not be the end of your journey of discovery but they will get you started confidently in the right direction.

GOLD RIBBED HARE'S EAR (GRHE) NYMPH

The use of hare's fur as a body material for artificial flies is as old as fly fishing. The texture means it is easily *dubbed* onto waxed tying thread and its barred, buff colouring is a great imitation of many natural nymphs, especially the olives and sedges.

Because no one would pick hare fur to imitate the smooth, transparent skin of a buzzer pupa it is hard to explain why a GRHE nymph often out-fishes super-glue coated artificial buzzers, the perfect imitations to our eyes, when buzzers are emerging. Perhaps the flat, gold tinsel provides a combination with the translucent, fuzzy fur that makes them irresistible. Who knows? It is important to shape the GRHE like a carrot with a wider thorax tapering back to a fine tail. This mimics the shape of most natural nymphs. The dressing below includes an additional rib of fine gold wire. The only reason for this is to strengthen the fly. Without it the trout's teeth rapidly break the gold tinsel and render the fly worthless. The fly's tail is tied using a few fibres of a natural, red game hackle. This seems to be important too.

There are fly dressers who will insist that the only fur that can be use to tie GRHE nymphs comes from the 'mask' i.e. the face or ears

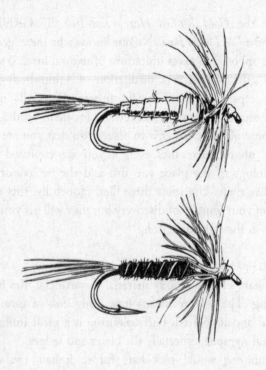

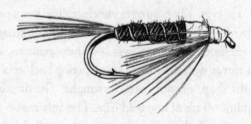

Fig. 34. The world's best nymphs.
Top: Gold-Ribbed Hare's Eye.
Middle: Cruncher.
Bottom: Red Diawl Bach.

of a hare, hence the name. The trout are not so choosy. If you decide to take up fly tying remember that a small patch of fur from a hare's body costs half the price of a mask.

This is one fly that also benefits hugely, when a little weight is required, by the addition of a small gold bead head when the fly is tied on a size 14 long shank hook to help exaggerate the nymph-like shape. A gold head provides a faster sinking fly, an attractive sink-and-lift retrieve and the extra flash. These may all play their part in attracting a trout including difficult fish that are concentrating on prey such as *Daphnia* or on tiny buzzers that are impossible to imitate.

One version of the GRHE is also a popular dry fly.

The clear message is that, tied in various forms and sizes, the GRHE is one fly you just cannot do without!

THE CRUNCHER

This nymph, like many other patterns, is tied with a body made using the feather fibre from a dark coloured, natural cock pheasant tail. The coppery colour of these feathers is a good imitation of the body colour of the free-swimming Lake and Pond Olive nymphs that hatch out in May.

The original *Pheasant Tail Nymph* (PTN) was made famous by Frank Sawyer over fifty years ago in his books on nymph fishing for chalk stream trout. The fly imitated a range of the dark brown *Ephemerid* nymphs that are found in these rivers. Later, Arthur Cove popularized a long shank pheasant tail nymph he used on the Midlands' trout reservoirs of the UK. Although this nymph had a bulbous thorax made from rabbit under fur to create a shape reminiscent of a buzzer pupa, Arthur often used to fish the pattern on large hooks that were bigger than most buzzers. He made it clear his pattern was 'representative' and not an exact imitation.

The Cruncher is a modern variation on this pheasant tail theme. The version below is a pretty good imitation of a Pond Olive nymph but it will catch trout at any time no matter what, if anything is happening on the insect front! Like several other nymph patterns it uses peacock hurl and natural, red game hackles.

RED DIAWL BACH

The original Diawl Bach fly was tied in Wales to imitate small beetles that fell onto the surface of upland lakes from the surrounding heather and bracken. The beetle-like body was tied using one or two strands of dark green, iridescent peacock herl (the single strands or 'barb' of the huge feathers that form a peacock's tail) ribbed with gold wire. The original is still a very effective fly. Recently it has been found to be equally good at fooling trout feeding on buzzer pupae, other insects or snails. A number of adaptations of the original have become popular. This is a red variant. Red can be a magic colour in trout flies. There is a red flash of haemoglobin when internal pressure splits the buzzer pupa's skin when an adult emerges. Perhaps this colour has become a feeding trigger. Who knows? A red varnished head completes the transformation. The natural, red game hackle (again!) tail and throat hackle of the original Diawl Bach pattern remain.

THE PATTERNS

The fly patterns detailed opposite are the recipe for any fly tier who is kind enough to tie these nymphs for you. Do not worry if you do not have such a friend. These flies, or very similar patterns, are available from any fly fishing tackle shop or website. No one can tell you why they are so successful. Something about them obviously 'triggers' a trout's interest and their movement says, 'I'm edible.'

	GRHE	Cruncher	Red Diawl Bach
Tying Thread	Olive	Brown	Red
Hook Sizes	14, 12 & LS14	10 to 16	
Tail	All natural, red game		
Tag	Fine, flat gold tinsel	None	
Rib	Fine gold wire	Fine copper wire	
Body	Hare's body fur	Pheasant tail fibres	Peacock herl
Thorax	Hare's body fur		Peacock herl
Hackle	Brown partridge	Natural red game throat hackle	
Head	Optional gold bead on LS14	None	Red varnish

OTHER IMITATIVE FLIES

If you know the three best nymphs in the world you might think you have no need for any other imitative flies nor for the chapters in this book that follow. That would miss the point of fly fishing!

At its heart, fly fishing is about observing the world of the trout and its prey. It demands an understanding of both what you see and of the vulnerability of the feeding trout. Your challenge is to exploit this weakness by offering a fly, and by fishing it in a way that imitates the prey and fools the fish.

If you find, by dint of experiment, that the best imitation is actually one of the nymphs described above that is fine, but do not stop looking. There is always a more effective fly, or way of fishing it, waiting to be discovered. What follows aims to help that quest.

SUMMARY

- The GRHE, Cruncher and Red Diawl Bach are 'generalist' nymphs that catch trout everywhere.
- They can be tied on hook sizes 10 to 16 to 'imitate' a wide range of trout's insect prey.
- Adding a gold bead head to the dressing of a GRHE creates a nymph with the weight to fish deeper in the water.
- There are also successful 'dry' and 'emerger' GRHE flies.
- The Cruncher successfully imitates the small dark nymphs of Pond Olives and many other *Ephemerid* species.
- The Red Diawl Bach is a successful fly when buzzers are emerging even though it is not a good imitation of buzzer pupae.

AND FINALLY

- When all else fails, use a floating line with a gold-head GRHE as the tail fly and a Red Diawl Bach as a dropper. Vary the retrieve. There is no better combination.

13
HOW?
USING IMITATIVE FLIES
SOLVING THE RIDDLES... SEEING THE CLUES
COMMON TROUT PREY AND HOW TO IMITATE THEM

On every day you go trout fishing, even if you are on a familiar water, the first trout is the most difficult to catch.

Trout are adaptable, carnivorous fish that will feed on whatever is available. It helps to know what is on their menu. You may see insects hatching, you may see active trout but it is easy to be mistaken about what they are eating until you have caught and killed your first fish and examined its stomach contents. It is amazing how many fly fishers fail to do this. They struggle for the rest of their day when the answer to the riddle is already in their bag.

You do not need to be an expert biologist to identify the stomach contents of a trout. All fishing tackle dealers sell *marrow spoons*, a tool first used by Victorian trout fishers to extract the contents of a trout's stomach. It is pushed horizontally down the dead fish's throat into its stomach, then twisted through half a turn before being extracted. Sometimes you need to do it twice to get everything. You can examine what is on the spoon (much of what is there will still be wriggling) but it is easier to identify what has been eaten if you shake the contents into a small polythene bag filled with water.

The food of choice of still water trout is *Daphnia*, the water flea. In a trout's stomach this just looks like green mush but shake it into water and you will see all the pinhead-sized individuals. Trout often feed exclusively on *Daphnia*. When this is happening you will struggle if you do not use a brightly-coloured lure and get it down to the right depth.

From March to mid-June, buzzers are the commonest insects in the stomachs of trout. The humped shape and striped bodies of buzzer pupae are unmistakable and you can immediately see what size and colour you need to imitate. Buzzers are such an important part of the trout's diet, especially in still waters, that catching buzzer-feeding trout merits a chapter in this book.

On small, heavily fished waters the commonest stomach contents may well be trout pellets. These waters are stocked daily to keep up trout numbers and these new fish are still digesting their last meal in the stock ponds. Such fish have never had to fend for themselves as all their food just sank gently through the water for them to mop up. It is no surprise that these fish are suckers for any fly that sinks slowly through the water. Their stomach contents also reveal their willingness to try anything they see. You will find small twigs, sections of plant, cigarette filter tips and anything else that looks like a trout pellet! But, do not forget they quickly learn what to avoid by seeing the mistakes their fellows make and within hours they can be ignoring nearly all the flies anglers throw at them. They quickly adapt to feeding naturally if there is a source, such as *Daphnia*, available.

The list of natural prey species that follows are the most common contents found in the stomachs of still water trout. This is not an exhaustive list and not all of these are found in all lakes and ponds. The waters you fish may have insect species or other prey in stomach contents that are not listed. Learning what they are, investigating how they behave and coming up with a plan to imitate them is exactly why looking at stomach contents is so important.

For example, adult Sedge Flies, their larvae and pupae are not mentioned because, although they are commonly seen in and on the water, they are surprisingly rare in the stomachs of trout. But, if the trout in your favourite water do happen to love Sedges, you have a rare opportunity to exploit.

Advice follows on what to do if you 'spoon' trout and discover they seem to be feeding on a particular prey.

If they are feeding on *Daphnia* or if they are newly stocked and are not yet feeding on natural prey, using a lure would be the obvious first choice.

As trout have catholic tastes many will have a variety of prey species in their stomachs. When you see this you can fish a variety of imitations, such as the GRHE, Cruncher or Red Diawl Bach with confidence. If one fly is not working, try another.

'Exact' imitation is not necessarily the answer. Fly tiers are constantly trying new imitations of well known trout prey. Some work better than others and all waters seem to have their favourite flies. The ideas below are only to get you started. Never stop experimenting.

THE FIRST CLUES

When you arrive at a trout venue you have never visited before there are some questions you need to ask. Whoever meets you or sells you your permit is a good person to start with. He or she should know what was caught the day before and what flies were successful. Listen carefully! What the trout did yesterday is the best clue on what they may do today.

You should try and find out where they were feeding and why. The trout converge into the areas they are finding food. For example, if a particular species of buzzer is hatching in April it may be emerging from a specific area and depth of water where its larvae live.

There are questions you can answer for yourself even if there is no one to help you.

Is the water 'fertile' and does it have enough dissolved calcium to support shell building prey like *Daphnia* and shrimps? If you see snails, it is 'fertile'. There will be plenty of plant growth and there will possibly be *Daphnia,* shrimps and water hog lice too. The trout have lots of choice of food and could be anywhere. You need to look for some other clues.

If there are no snails it is 'infertile', which means that small insect species and 'terrestrials' will be the major food source for trout. You can be confident all the trout will be in shallow water.

WHAT CAN YOU SEE HAPPENING?

If trout are feeding within a foot of the surface you will be able to see them rising. What do the rises tell you? Take time to look. Swirling rises mean they are chasing fast moving prey. Or are they cruising about in a leisurely manner? This means they are eating stationary prey that cannot escape.

If you are fishing one of the small, gin clear lakes common in southern England, sight fishing is the order of the day. You keep still, look out for a patrolling trout, work out its depth and choose an ambush point where you can drop a suitably weighted fly.

Even if the water you have chosen is bigger, cloudy and the fish are more difficult to see, it pays to spend time looking before you start. It is never wasted.

ARE FISH RISING?

Feeding-trout near the surface do not usually make a fuss about it. They will 'head-and-tail' for stationary food just under the surface or just 'sip' it down if it is right in the surface film.

A single rise does not tell you much. A trout leaping clear of the water is a fish in distress!

What you want to see is an individual fish rising again and again as it follows a determined path. Even better is a small shoal of trout which are showing repeatedly, presumably all concentrating on the same food source at the same depth not far below the surface.

DRY FLY FISHING

Many fly fishers speak of dry fly fishing using floating flies on the water surface in mystical terms.

The reason for this is historical. In the last quarter of the nineteenth century a cult for 'dry fly fishing only' emerged on the glorious and exclusive Hampshire chalk streams. This, coupled with a Victorian passion for insect taxonomy and 'matching-the-hatch', spawned the myth that superior skills were also needed to fish a dry fly. They are not!

Some fly fishers become obsessed with dry fly fishing and insist on trying it as their first tactic in almost all conditions and everywhere they fish. Of course, there is a lot of attraction to dry fly fishing. It is a highly visual art. The fly sits on top of the water and you see the trout rise and sip it down. The flies have to be cleverly tied and delicately presented. And, on its day, a dry fly approach can produce devastating results.

There is an obvious reason for this. All trout, no matter their origin or where they live, become used to insects alighting on, rising to or being blown on to the water. While they are in, or on, the surface film they are not wholly visible as they would be underwater so the trout is reacting to the impression the insect or artificial fly makes on the surface film. If they are feeding eagerly, they are not usually very selective. Trout that have learned to avoid bright lures and artificial nymphs and 'wet' flies under the surface are often still quick and eager to rise to, and take, any surface 'fly' they see.

All river fishers, and a lot of still water dry fly experts, use only one dry fly on the end of their leader and tippet. There is no point in casting a long way as you need to see, and keep in touch with, your fly. This usually means casting repeatedly which is no bad thing as trout often take a fly they see alighting on the water.

You sometimes have to choose the right pattern of fly, especially on rivers, but many still water fishers depend on very few pattern. Patterns such as Big Red, Midas and various Hoppers are popular.

The dressing of these flies is important. They must sit 'in' rather than 'on' the surface film and usually a lot of the hackles under the body of the fly are cut away so that it sits down in the surface. Modern proprietary treatments such as silicon-based 'Gink' or spray-on powders are used to ensure the flies float. They all need drying (paper kitchen towel is good) and re-treatment after a time or catching a fish.

The commonest reason a trout swirls at, but rejects, a dry fly is because the tippet to which it is attached is floating. The trout reacts to the small impression of the fly in the surface film but refuses it if it seems to be attached to a long snaking length of line. Dry fly fishers obsessively treat their leaders to ensure they sink. Nothing does this better than a paste made by mixing Fuller's Earth with washing-up liquid.

The ultimate skill in dry fly fishing is accurate casting. In rivers, trout hold station and a fly has to be accurately cast so that it enters their line of sight without being dragged away unnaturally by an awkward wind or current. On still waters dry flies are usually cast downwind, left 10 seconds and cast again while you constantly search for a rising fish to aim at. This is not as easy as it sounds. On still waters, active fish tend to swim up-wind looking for food. If you cast at a rise you have seen you'll inevitably be behind your quarry. The secret is to cast 2 or 3 metres up-wind of any rise. The trout will soon get there!

This technique demands lots of concentration. Trout sip down dry flies very gently and this is so easy to miss, especially on a lake where you have been fishing 'blind' in a decent ripple and seeing no rises for a long time. Everyone tries to see their flies on the surface but this is often impossible, The trick is to concentrate on the patch of water beyond the tip of your floating fly line. This is a good reason for keeping your leader fairly short (no more than 3 metres) and, if you are using more than one fly, to tie the droppers no more than 1 metre apart. If you see a rise, strike! It will inevitably have risen to your fly. You do have to strike firmly when dry fly fishing. The line will not be tight and trout seem able to spit out a fly instantly if they are not happy about it.

As ever, practice makes perfect. But, do not worry, you'll learn quickly.

WHEN NO FISH ARE RISING

If there is absolutely no surface activity it does not mean they are not feeding. It just means there is little reason for fishing artificial flies close to the surface. Remember that trout hate changing depth. They could be gorging on buzzer pupae, for example, and if they are feeding 2 metres down there will not be sign of it on the surface. Are there adult buzzers around you? Can you see smoke-like trails of them in the lee of nearby trees? Is it April or May? If so, buzzer imitations fished deep would be a wise start.

WHERE SHOULD YOU START FISHING?

Obviously, if you can see trout feeding you should target them. If there is no sign of any activity think about what you can do to lower the odds. Try to formulate a plan.

What is the weather doing? Bright, hot days are likely to push the fish into deeper water. Windy days may deliver terrestrial insects on the upwind shore. If there is no sign of such feeding, do not forget that winds create a sub-surface current in still waters and that rainbow trout love to cruise against this current, especially if they are finding food in the surface layers. It may pay to fish from the end of any headland where a crosswind allows you to retrieve your flies across such a current.

It is also possible that an onwind shore may concentrate food which has drifted across to it or is being dislodged by the waves. But, remember trout avoid cloudy, muddy water where their vision will be restricted. In short, do not just choose a spot at random.

If your chosen location produces no fish after twenty minutes, move onto plan B. If whatever you are doing is not working, do something different.

Are other fishers catching fish? Never be slow to move to an area where fish are obviously feeding. Every clue is welcome. A pair of binoculars can be an indispensable tool.

Despite your best efforts what you see can sometimes be downright misleading. This is why the first trout is the hardest to catch.

So when you catch one do not fail to examine its stomach contents. It provides the best intelligence of all. Here is what you may find and what to do.

DAPHNIA FEEDERS

If your first trout has a stomach full of *Daphnia* and nothing else, then *Daphnia* is available in abundance. You can bet that this is the prey all the trout are concentrating on. They are unlikely to be diverted from this easy feast by artificial nymphs or dry flies. You should use a lure... and a pretty garish one at that! A fluorescent Orange Blob is a good start. You have to experiment to find the right depth. The trout will be cruising at the same depth as the *Daphnia*. The best retrieve is a long smooth draw. If trout are moving close to the surface on a dull day, then that is where to start. If it is bright and sunny, the *Daphnia* are likely to be further down and it may be worth experimenting with intermediate and other sinking lines.

If the trout's stomach contains *Daphnia* and other food such as buzzer pupae it means that the *Daphnia* bloom is not as abundant and that the fish are more likely to take imitative flies. However, the chances are that they are prospecting at the depth where they are also finding *Daphnia*. You need to find that depth and then you can be confident your fly, and it may not matter much what pattern you have chosen, will be taken.

BUZZER FEEDERS

If your first trout has a stomach full of buzzers it tells you the size and colour of the buzzer pupae hatching that day. Chapter 14 describes a range of successful tactics.

When you find a 'mixed bag' of insects, including buzzer pupae in your first trout, it again tells you that the fish are prospecting. No prey species is so abundant that the trout have become 'selective' feeders. It may also provide clues about the best depth to try. Have any of the buzzers or other insects got wings? If so, do not go deep. On the other hand, if there are also shrimps, water hog lice or snails (all of which live on the bottom) in the mix, then get your flies down close to the bottom too.

DAMSELFLY FEEDERS

Throughout the summer months most trout stomachs contain at least one damselfly nymph. Sometimes they contain nothing else! This is a sure sign that the nymphs are available in large numbers and some are swimming to the surface to emerge. A damselfly nymph imitation is obviously the fly to start with.

The nymphs are strong swimmers and if the trout are taking them near the surface you should see some 'swirling' rises as trout accelerate to catch them, often above or close to the protective weed beds where the nymphs have been living. If you see such activity, a damsel imitation with a buoyant head, e.g. small 'eyes' formed of *plastazote* can be very useful. The buoyancy keeps the artificial close to the surface film. It can be cast and retrieved above weed beds where a sinking imitation would immediately get hung up.

If there is no sign of surface activity, then try fishing deeper but cast close to features such as overhanging bushes, emerging plants and other structures which the nymphs use to crawl out of the water to wait for their skin to split and for a new adult to emerge. It is useful to have damselfly imitations of different 'weight' to help

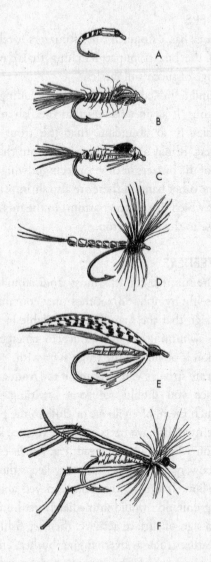

Fig. 35. Imitative flies.
A: Buzzer pupa. B: Damselfly nymph. C: Mayfly nymph. D: Mayfly dun.
E: Fry imitation. F: Daddy-Long-Legs.

you explore at different depths. Many imitations have plastic or glass eyes which add some weight. The heaviest incorporate gold bead heads. Again, sensible tweaks to a single fly pattern will dictate the speed of sinking, the depth at which it fishes and its 'action' during the retrieve.

Most artificial damsel nymphs are olive-green in colour to match the natural insect. Those in your first trout's stomach will tell you if this is the right colour. In some waters damselfly nymphs tend to be a darker green colour or even brownish. It pays to imitate this local colour.

When natural damselflies swim they waggle their body like a small fish's tail so most imitations incorporate a 'tail' of marabou feather fibres to provide a similar motion. The nymphs swim in short bursts and then seem to rest so a 'figure-of-eight' or stop-start retrieve is best. Varying the gaps between movements, so that the artificial seems to stop and then sink towards the bottom, imitates the behaviour of the natural. Trout often take damsel nymphs 'on the drop'.

Trout stomach contents show they find damsel nymphs to eat even when they are not emerging *en masse*. This is the reason that an artificial damselfly nymph is one of the must-have flies of the summer.

The most obvious evidence of the abundance of damselfly nymphs is the welcome sight of the bright blue adults that are such an obvious part of waterside wild life through the summer.

At Elinor Trout Fishery near Kettering there are thousands of damselflies. A feature of the summer trout fishing here is the fact that the trout even take adult damselflies hungrily if they fall onto the surface and the lucky, local anglers catch them using beautiful, exact imitations. This feeding pattern does not happen everywhere. Look out for it!

MAYFLY FEEDERS

If you are lucky enough to fish where there is a good population of Mayflies (*Ephemeroptera danica*) then you can bet that, from mid-

May right into August, both the nymphs and the adults will be found in trout stomachs. When there is a big hatch they will contain nothing else.

The creamy-coloured Mayfly nymphs swim and crawl up from their larval tubes in the muddy margins of lakes and ponds to emerge as adults. The nymphs are 20 mm long and trout soon feed selectively on them when a good 'hatch' starts. They tend to emerge from 11 am until the afternoon. Trout may be taking nymphs below the surface before the adults are obvious. There are several patterns of artificial Mayfly nymphs to choose from.

Unlike buzzers, Mayfly adults do not emerge instantly when a nymph reaches the surface. It takes time for the nymph's skin to split and for the first-stage adult or *dun* to get its body out and for its wings to dry a little so that it can take flight. This is a vulnerable time and trout can rise enthusiastically to take these 'emergers'. You do not need to examine stomach contents to see this is happening. Do not delay in getting a Mayfly 'emerger' pattern (there are several and they all work) onto the end of your leader.

Later, and always in the late evening, the sexually mature, female, second stage adults known as the *imago* or *spinner* return to lay their eggs and to die. These now shiny-skinned insects end up floating helplessly in the surface film with their wings extended. Again there are many 'spinner' fly patterns, all of which fool the trout who cruise just under the surface, sipping them down leisurely until well after dark.

Many trout waters have no Mayflies. Perhaps surprisingly, on many of these waters an artificial Mayfly nymph is a popular local fly. It is simply a good white 'lure' for trout that have never seen the real thing. This is a reminder never to become precious about the choice of artificial flies. Only rarely does success depend on exact imitations of trout prey.

TROUT FEEDING ON 'OLIVES'

There are a number of species of *Ephemeroptera sp.* or 'up-wing' flies in lakes, lochs and ponds across the UK. They are all smaller than their Mayfly cousins. Trout anglers usually call them 'olives'. The greatest variety of species occurs in the less fertile upland waters. If you are interested in identifying the different species you see, there are plenty of reference books to help. Artificial olives are usually tied on size 12 or 14 hooks.

Traditional, artificial 'wet flies' that have been used by loch fishermen for generations were originally created to imitate olives. Nearly all imitate the classic up-wing shape. These flies come in hundreds of colour variations, some of which imitate a recognizable insect, but many bear no resemblance to anything that ever flew. This does not mean they have not stood the test of time and you can be sure they all work occasionally.

The commonest still water olive, especially in more fertile, lowland waters, is the Pond Olive which hatches in late April and May. Like Mayflies, duns emerge when their nymphs swim to the surface where their skin splits to reveal this first stage adult. Because the adult flies struggle to take off, you often first realize what is happening when you see a flotilla of adults, with sail-like wings catching the wind, drifting across the water.

Still water trout prefer to feed on the fast moving nymphs, which are particularly vulnerable as they swim to the surface, rather than the drifting adults. Trout do take the emerging adults right in the surface film but, as they prefer the nymphs, you may find they are concentrated in a small area where the nymphs are emerging and they are not following the surviving adults as they drift away. Trout often chase the nymphs with gusto. You see 'bulging' swirling rises in the feeding area as fast moving trout take the nymphs a foot or so below the surface. These nymphs are dark brown and easily imitated. Use flies such as the Cruncher or Sawyer's Pheasant Tail Nymph (PTN).

If a trout's stomach is full of small dark brown nymphs but you can see no surface activity, this means the fish are taking them close to the bottom, perhaps in deeper water. Use an imitation fly that is heavy (e.g. dressed on a heavy hook or using thicker copper wire).

If you do see that the trout are concentrating on sipping down the emerging adults from the surface, perhaps because the supply of nymphs has dried up as the emergence comes to an end, it is time to switch to a dry fly or emerger pattern on or in the surface film. Use a dry Gold-Ribbed Hare's Ear (GRHE) fly tied Klinkhammer style or one on a normal hook with any hackle chopped away below the body so that it lies right in the surface film. Just cast the fly into the feeding area and leave it. Pond Olives need time to dry out before they can fly away. They do not move and just drift before the wind.

Other species of olives have lighter coloured nymphs and are smaller than Pond Olives. Gold-Ribbed Hare's Ear nymphs of an appropriate size are always a good bet.

TROUT FEEDING ON WATER BOATMEN (CORIXA SP.)

These freshwater beetles (yes, they have wings, breathe air and can fly away!) build up to big numbers in many lakes and ponds in the course of a summer. They are named after their long, oar-like front legs and their distinctive, paddling movement. They float upwards if they stop paddling. They do this from time to time so that they can take aboard a bubble of air under their wing cases to keep them going as they dive down to feed.

As weed growth dies away in the autumn their cover disappears and they become more and more vulnerable to trout predation. Sometimes in September and October the examination of trout stomach contents will show that the fish are feeding on them exclusively.

Two excellent imitations of water boatmen, usually tied on size 10 or 12 hooks, are a Hare's Ear Nymph pattern tied with silver tinsel or a Silver Invicta, a traditional wet fly. They both have silver tinsel at the rear of their bodies which imitates the air bubble they carry. Get the size of this artificial right... this is how examining stomach contents helps... and you will have no trouble catching these trout if you use a slow 'stop-start' retrieve. To be honest, you will probably find an everyday GRHE nymph works just as well but it is fun to think that one with a butt of silver gives you an edge!

FISH FRY FEEDERS

In upland, unfertile waters the only coarse fish populations are perch and minnows. Perch fry are targeted by trout beside weed beds in mid-summer in some years but not in others. It probably depends on how successful spawning was and whether large shoals of fry are unable to find enough cover in the weed beds.

Minnows only figure as an occasional item in trout stomachs. Minnows always remain in the shallowest water and are not usually vulnerable to trout predation.

In contrast, there are sometimes huge populations of the fry of other coarse fish, typically roach or rudd, in some fertile, lowland lakes. Trout home in on these fry just after they hatch out from their eggs in June and again in the autumn when the weed growth dies back and the grown-on fry, which are now 5 cm long, become exposed to predation again.

In both cases, trout feeding on fry usually reveal themselves by very visible, splashy rises close to weed beds or other 'structures'. Seagulls sometimes join in! The trout, often feeding in loose shoals, violently herd the fry against this structure before slashing into them. They then return, in a more leisurely manner, to mop up any stunned casualties hanging in the surface.

Anglers often refer to newly hatched fry as *jelly* fry because this is what a trout stomach full of them looks like. They are mostly transparent with an obvious pair of black and silver eye balls. They are tiny, only 5 mm long, and a good artificial needs to be nothing more than some pearl tinsel wrapped round the shank of a size 14 hook tied in with black silk dotted with two spots of white varnish to represent eyes.

Imitations of the grown-on fry of autumn are usually close imitations of the real thing and there are plenty of fry patterns to choose from. The best ones float in, or even better, hang in the surface film. The best tactic is to cast them out into a feeding area and then not to move them. Trout expect to see stunned fry! If a trout swirls at an imitation and does not take it, a sudden, short and fast retrieve can often induce a savage take.

TROUT FEEDING ON TERRESTRIAL FLIES

From mid-summer onwards, terrestrial adult insects blown onto the surface of lakes, lochs and ponds become an ever more important part of a trout's diet. In the most infertile, upland waters, trout may be absolutely dependent on them as examination of their stomach contents will reveal.

Happily, these insects are not difficult to imitate. Most of them are black and shiny. This is why so many successful traditional wet flies are predominately black with a touch of silver. Examples are the Black Pennell and the Zulu. These are still excellent imitations of drowned adult flies and beetles when fished below the surface and therefore do well on windy days.

Today, many trout fishers prefer to use a dry fly that is fished on the surface. A Black Hopper is an obvious choice. There are also several popular dry fly patterns that aim to be exact imitations of the Hawthorn Fly which is found around lowland lakes in May/June or the similar red-legged Heather Fly which is blown onto upland lakes and lochs out of the surrounding heather in August. These fly dressings, and those of modern beetle imitations, often incorporate black *plastozote* foam which increases their buoyancy.

Do not be dismayed if you have not got an exact imitation of a terrestrial fly that you see trout are feeding on. Remember that there are hundreds of species of land flies blown onto lakes throughout the summer and a few Black or Claret Hopper patterns tied onto hook sizes 12 and 14 will imitate nearly all of them.

Trout cannot hide the fact that they are taking terrestrial flies from the surface. But they do sip them down very delicately and you sometimes have to watch the water and floating insects very carefully to see them. Trout often patrol the line where an off-shore wind first begins to ripple the surface but, in fact, floating flies are likely to be sipped down wherever they are found by patrolling trout. While brown trout are likely to patrol a productive area, rainbow trout seem to prefer to travel a long distance in small shoals, moving up-wind as if they are swimming up a river. When shore fishing a brown trout loch in the Highlands you are better to keep on the move in the search for feeding brown trout but on a rainbow trout water it is often a better bet to position yourself at the end of any headland or promontory on a shore that the wind is blowing along and wait for the trout to come to you.

Terrestrial flies are doomed when they land on water and if it is windy they will quickly drown and sink. So your imitation flies do not need to be moved after casting out. It does not matter if they sink unless there is a very heavy fall of naturals and the trout are selectively feeding on floating flies. If they are, this will soon be obvious as they will ignore artificials that have sunk below the surface.

DADDY-LONG-LEGS

There is one common terrestrial insect that is neither black nor small and is much loved by trout. Daddy-Long-Legs or Crane Flies come in several species and are commonest on lakes and ponds that adjoin pasture land. The numbers vary wildly from year to year. Their larvae, known as Leather Jackets, live in the soil of grass fields and the adults emerge, sometimes in large numbers, in the late summer usually peaking in September.

'Daddies' are poor flyers and on any breezy day when they are emerging, some will inevitably be deposited onto the surface of nearby lakes and ponds. Trout love'em!

There are many artificial Daddy fly patterns. They all work but choose one where the hackle is cut down so that as much of the body and the trailing legs as possible are in the surface film. If the trout are swirling under your artificial and not taking it, attack it with your scissors to remove whatever is holding it above the surface film. It is amazing how delicately a trout can sip down such a large fly so watch it very carefully indeed. If you have lost sight of it, strike if you see a 'sip' where you think it might be.

This is an excellent rule-of-thumb when fishing with dry flies on still waters. You should fish dry flies using a short leader (2 to 3 metres) so that by watching the tip of the floating line you have a good idea where your fly is a couple of metres or so beyond it. Small dry flies are difficult to see so, unless it is very obvious, do not try. Just concentrate on the square metre or so in which you know your fly sits and react to any trout 'sip' you see. Inevitably the fish will have taken your fly.

UNSELECTIVE FEEDERS – WHEN STOMACH CONTENTS ARE A MIXED BAG

Most of the trout stomachs you sample will contain several prey species. This tells you that the trout are not feeding hard and selectively on a single vulnerable prey. You know what to do... get out the world's best nymphs! You may still have some work to do to find the best feeding depth.

Most trout eating a variety of prey species are simply 'grazing' and searching out any available food. Look first for clues about their favoured feeding depth.

If a stomach has a mixture of hog lice, shrimps, snails, perhaps the odd damselfly nymph or baby fish but no *Daphnia* you can be pretty sure it is grazing close to the bottom over stones and weeds where all these prey live. You could fish a lure and use an intermediate or sinking line to get down there. Or, try a 'general' weighted fly like a gold-head GRHE nymph on a floating line. The trout are not being choosy so it will not matter much which fly pattern you use.

If there are *Daphnia* present with other prey such as nymphs and buzzer pupae, you can be sure the trout has been grazing further up in open water. It has been searching for *Daphnia,* always the favourite, but taking any other prey it sees. The presence of some *Daphnia* will be dictating its favoured depth and you will have to do more experimentation to find it. But, you do not have to get right down to the bottom. Use a lure or unweighted nymphs and an intermediate line to explore different depths. Change to a floating line if you find that the trout are not far down.

A trout that has been eating adult flies among a mixed bag has been prospecting close to the surface. You are probably seeing other fish rising too. Obviously you should use a floating line and make sure that your flies are un-weighted and tied on lightweight hooks so that they are not sinking too deep.

NO VISUAL CLUES? AN EMPTY STOMACH?

Finally, what do you do if you have struggled to catch your first trout, having seen no visual clues, and then find that its stomach is empty?

There is no easy answer. Rainbow trout are eating machines and even newly stocked, well-fed trout from the fish farm experiment by eating anything they see floating around in their new environment such as twigs and pieces of plants. If their stomachs are empty there is a serious shortage of prey. This is a common situation in small heavily stocked ponds or if rainbow trout are stocked into barren, upland waters.

Your best bet is to use an intermediate or slow sinking line and lures to explore water between 1 and 3 metres in depth. Rainbow trout that cannot find food seek out water of this depth and tend to stay fairly close to the bottom. This is where you should fish your fly. A black lure would be a good start. Use a buoyant Booby on a short leader if you find that you are getting snagged on the bottom.

Wild brown trout are more at home in unfertile waters. Their sole source of food is insects. In the spring it will be mostly buzzers and olives. Adult terrestrial insects become their dominant food source as the summer advances. Brown trout have the ability to switch off completely if no insects are hatching or being blown onto the water, perhaps as a means of saving energy. Experiments show they are much more active for the few hours after dawn and before dusk. This is when to concentrate your effort if the going is tough. All you can do on a brown trout fishery where the water seems 'dead' is to home in on those shallow areas where brown trout find their food. In upland lakes this is close to the rocky shores that shelter their prey. Avoid sandy and gravel bottoms where there is no shelter for insects.

On all trout waters, no matter if you are chasing brown or rainbow trout, when no trout are rising you know there is no point in fishing very close to the surface. Experimentation is the key. Search different places, fish at different depths, use different flies and try different speeds of retrieve. If what you are doing is not working after ten minutes, do something different.

Hopefully, you finally catch a trout. Bang it on the head and see what it has been eating. With luck, this one will tell you what to do next.

SUMMARY

EXAMINE AND IMITATE THE TROUT STOMACH CONTENTS

- *Daphnia* only: Put on an orange lure. Experiment to find the depth.
- Buzzer pupae only: Imitate the colour. Experiment to find depth.
- Damselfly Nymphs only: Imitate the colour. Fish shallow.
- Mayfly Nymphs only: Imitate them. Start deep but expect emerging adults by lunchtime.
- Olive Nymphs only: Imitate them. Start fishing mid-water and expect emerging adults soon.
- Water Boatmen only: Imitate them using a Silver Invicta or a Hare's Ear Nymph.
- Small Fish only: Imitate their size. Find the feeding location beside a weed bed or structure.
- Adult Terrestrial Insects: Imitate their size and colour with a stationary fly 'in' the surface film.
- A 'mixed-bag' including hog lice, snails or shrimps: Fish deep.
- A 'mixed-bag' including *Daphnia*: Fish mid-water but keep experimenting.
- A 'mixed-bag' including adult insects: Fish close to the surface.
- An empty stomach: Try a black lure close to the bottom in 2 metres of water. Keep experimenting!

14

HOW?
USING IMITATIVE FLIES
CATCHING TROUT FEEDING ON BUZZERS

The insect genus Chironomus sp. or 'non-biting midges' are the most abundant insects found in lakes, ponds and reservoirs across the world. UK fly fishers know them as 'buzzers'. They emerge in every month of the year, from both 'fertile' and 'infertile', upland waters, albeit in smaller numbers. Sometimes, but especially in late spring, they emerge in spectacular numbers in fertile lakes. At these times trout feed selectively on buzzer pupae to the exclusion of all else. That is why the fly fisher needs to know how to imitate them and the tactics to try.

The life-cycle of buzzers is *egg>larva>pupa>flying adult*. This life-cycle is similar to that of many other common insect species but contrasts with the *egg>nymph>dun>imago* cycle of Mayflies and olives.

Buzzers are most vulnerable to trout and coarse fish predation at the pupa stage in their life-cycle. The pupae emerge from the larval tubes they form in muddy bottoms and float slowly up to the surface. Here, the pupa's skin splits and a fully formed adult emerges. They are able to fly off at once. This is one reason why buzzer 'hatches' are not as easy to see as hatches of other insects. If you watch carefully you will see individual adults rising from the water surface but you will not see squadrons of them floating away on the wind. The best indication is often the activity of flocks of swallows, martins and swifts working close to the surface of the water. On Grafham Water in Cambridgeshire even the local black-headed gulls have learnt to feed on emerging buzzers. They are also

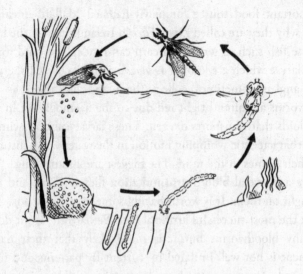

Fig. 36. Life-cycle of buzzers.

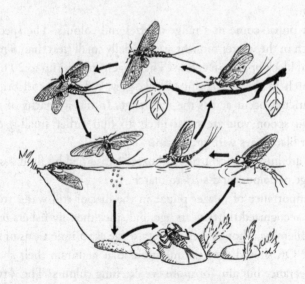

Fig. 37. Life-cycle of Mayflies and olives.

an important food source for newly-hatched Mallard ducklings. This is why they are called *Duck Flies* in Ireland. Follow the birds!

Coarse fish such as tench and carp can root in the mud for the buzzer larvae which are known as *bloodworms* by coarse fishermen. These anglers sometimes collect them and use them as bait. Bloodworms are often bright red due to the haemoglobin in their body fluids that transports oxygen. These larvae cannot swim but have a characteristic whipping motion in the water when disturbed from their homes in the mud. The biggest are 20 mm long.

There are several bloodworm imitation flies available and trout are caught on them. It is worth having some in your fly box. They are not the most successful artificial flies. Perhaps the trout do not see many bloodworms but it is more likely that their natural movement is not well imitated by current fly patterns and this is why they do not trigger the hoped-for response. There is a chance here for experimental fly dressers to come up with a 'magic' imitation.

Buzzer pupae come in a range of sizes and colours. The species that hatch in the winter months are normally small (less than 6 mm long) and black or grey in colour. The biggest species (up to 20 mm long) hatch in the late spring. Black, grey, red, olive and bright green varieties occur across the size range. In the stomachs of the trout you spoon you are most likely to find either small green pupae or black ones with grey stripes.

There are hundreds of artificial buzzer pupae tied by fly dressers in a range of colours and sizes to match.

The importance of buzzer pupae in the diet of still water trout was first recognized thirty years ago and since then fly fishers have faced a dilemma. Should they attempt to tie exact imitations of the naturals? Or, should they tie imitations that maintain their shape and appearance but aim for more eye-catching colours? The jury is still out on this and the experiments continue.

Early buzzer pupae imitations copied their outline shape and had no hackles or 'wings' like traditional flies. Their bodies were fatter than the natural pupa because fly dressers used materials like seal's fur and peacock feather herl.

Today, most buzzer pupae imitations are very slim to imitate the real thing.

They are also brushed over with epoxy or 'hard-as-nails' varnish (available wherever fly tying gear is sold) to mimic the transparent cuticle of the pupae. One advantage is that varnished buzzers are streamlined and heavy so they sink quickly. There are, and will continue to be, endless experiments with colour. Some fly dressers concentrate on achieving exact imitations using modern holographic tinsels ribbed with thread while others try quirky combinations such as a black body with a fluorescent, lime green thorax, quite unlike anything found in nature.

They all fool trout at times!

This dilemma is nothing new. Over a hundred years ago, the fly fishers who fished the chalk streams of southern England came to believe that only exact imitations of the floating flies they saw trout eating would fool the sophisticated, 'educated' trout that had grown big by avoiding angler's flies. No one can deny that exact imitations of insects should and do catch trout but, as we do not have a trout's eyes or brain, who can tell exactly what pushes their buttons?

There is another more important consideration. Buzzer pupae emerge in their millions during a hatch so a trout has plenty of choice. The perfect 'imitation' from the fly fisher's point of view is one that stands out like a beacon in the crowd and which, for some reason, is sought out by a feeding trout.

Listen to expert advice at your local water and always experiment to find the best buzzer imitation on the day. Three good examples are detailed here.

THREE GREAT BUZZER PATTERNS

	Red	Black	Green
Hook Size	12 or 14	8 to 14	14 to 16
Tying Thread	Black	Black	Olive
Tail	None		
Rib	Red holographic tinsel	Fine silver wire	Olive Kevlar thread
Body	Black thread	Black thread	Grey floss silk
Thorax	As above with orange swan herl cheeks	Orange floss silk	Yellow floss silk
Head	Varnished tying thread Brush with three coats of varnish		

HOW TO FISH BUZZER IMITATIONS – USING A FLOATING LINE

Buzzer larvae live in mud in water at all depths but the biggest populations are found in water which is between 2 and 4 metres deep. A few species live in shallower water and some are found in very deep water indeed. Even in the biggest lakes, whether they are deep or shallow, regular fly fishers know about buzzer 'holes', often areas where the water is deeper than the surrounding area and where the bottom is muddy. These are the places where the biggest populations of larvae are found. This is where it pays to concentrate your efforts when buzzers are emerging.

There are many different species of buzzers which emerge at different times of the year. Try to tap into the local 'experts'

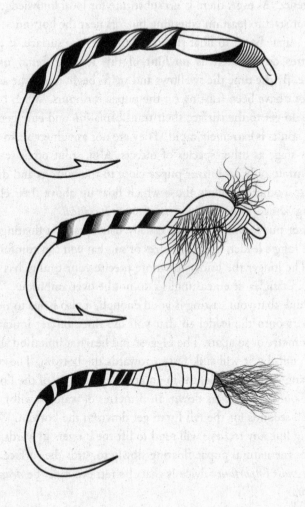

Fig. 38. Three buzzer imitations.
These flies are tied in many colours and on various hook types and sizes.

network and keep a diary. You need to anticipate buzzer emergence. As ever, there is no substitute for local knowledge.

Trout start to feast on emerging buzzers near the bottom as soon as the pupae begin to float slowly up towards the surface. If this is 3 metres down, there is no hint of this feeding frenzy on the surface. By the time the swallows and swifts begin to eat the adults, the trout have been feasting on the pupae for hours. When buzzer pupae do get to the surface their transformation and emergence as flying adults is extremely rapid. They are not as vulnerable to trout at this stage as other species of insects. Also, trout often seem to concentrate only on buzzer pupae close to the bottom and do not seem to bother to follow those which float up above their chosen feeding 'zone'. *Fishing at the 'right' depth is critical.*

Buzzer pupae imitations are usually fished using a floating line. Use as long a leader, up to 5 metres or so, that you can comfortably cast. The longer the leader the more precise your timing has to be to avoid tangles when casting, so do not be over ambitious. When you think that your casting is good enough, it also helps to tie two droppers onto the leader so that you use three buzzer imitations, each a metre or so apart. The biggest and heaviest imitation should be the tail fly. It will sink fastest towards the bottom. The others will hang at different depths in an arc below the tip of the floating line. Count the buzzers down. In 3 metres of water it will take at least 30 seconds for the tail fly to get down to the bottom. With a floating line any retrieve will tend to lift the buzzers upwards. This mimics the natural pupae floating slowly towards the surface.

The *most important* advice is that the retrieve must be *dead slow and stop*.

Buzzer pupae rise vertically to the surface. They cannot swim horizontally. Time and time again you will see fly fishers fishing buzzer imitations with a rapid 'stop-start' or 'figure-of-eight' retrieve which means they are racing horizontally through the water. They do not catch many trout. On heavily fished waters trout soon learn to avoid buzzers fished in this way. They can still be tempted by one that is stationary.

Do not forget that you are not limited to buzzer pupae imitations. At times you can do better using a GRHE or a Red Diawl Bach. It pays to mix-and-match. And, if one particular fly is out fishing the others, put three of them on.

If the wind direction allows, always try to fish in a light crosswind. You cast out, tighten the line and let the buzzers sink. By the time the tail fly is well down, this ripple will be stretching the floating line into a gentle arc. All you need to do is to keep in touch as the flies are slowly dragged round. You may need to 'mend' the line by flicking the rod tip to straighten out the bow in the line forming in the wind to slow it down. Retrieve extremely slowly, just to keep in touch, and the line tight, until you need to re-cast. Sometimes any retrieve can be too fast. You may need to cast at an angle to the wind and to the ripple to enable you to remain in touch but to minimize the movement of the flies. This is the reason many fly fishers refer to this technique as 'straight-line buzzer fishing'.

When a trout takes a buzzer fished in this way, the take or *pull* is usually confident and solid. As long as you react by clamping the fly line against the rod handle with your index finger and keep the rod pointing down the line, the trout will hook itself.

USING A SINKING LINE

Sometimes, especially during a hot spell with high water temperatures, trout retreat to the depths of a lake where they continue to feed on buzzer pupae. They can then be difficult to fool on anything else. It is almost impossible to fish buzzer imitations in water more that 3 metres deep using a floating line. The surface movements and wind work against the right presentation even if you are able to cast using the longest leader.

Using a sinking line gets the buzzer imitations down but another problem is created. If the line is down at the same depth as the flies, any movement of the line, even with the slowest retrieve, means the flies move horizontally rather than vertically like the natural pupae. The partial solution to this problem is to use a buoyant tail fly, normally a Booby, which effectively suspends buzzer imitations on droppers above the bottom with the leader arcing up from the line. It also enables the essential 'dead slow and stop' retrieve. Without the buoyant tail fly the heavy imitations snag the bottom and cannot be fished slowly enough.

You still need to discover the depth the trout prefer and to count the sinking line down to this depth. A fast sinking line can be left to go right down so that it rests on the bottom. The buoyant tail fly keeps the buzzers just above it. A more slowly sinking line, which is usually a better option, makes it easier to explore different depths and to keep the retrieve under control when the right depth is found.

A slow retrieve of buzzer imitations using a sinking line can only be achieved from the bank or from a firmly anchored boat.

And, happily, the trout may find the Booby more enticing than the buzzer imitations.

FISHING BUZZERS UNDER A 'BUNG'

Over the last few years a new, and very successful, way to fish buzzer imitations using a floating line has been developed. It is a method that best exploits the success factors detailed above.

Fly fishers discovered that if they replace their top dropper fly with a floating fly and allow a couple of buzzer imitations to hang below it, they create three immediate advantages. Firstly, the buzzer imitations become static as they settle at their suspended depth and any movement of the floating fly on the top dropper results in vertical movements of the buzzers. Secondly, the imitations are fished at different depths so at least one of them is likely to be at the 'right' depth. Thirdly, a take means the floating fly suddenly disappears... it acts just like a coarse fisher's float... the perfect bite indicator!

It did not take long for the floating dry fly to be replaced with proprietary, more buoyant, brightly coloured 'bungs' which could be fixed on the leader close to its junction with the tip of the fly line. Three, or even four, buzzer imitations of different sizes and colours on droppers below the bung mean lots of options are covered.

On hard fished still waters where the trout have 'wised up' it can be the only way to succeed. On less heavily fished waters, where a naive trout may still take a buzzer imitation behaving unnaturally, most experts still rate fishing under a bung as between five and ten times more successful than fishing with the straight-line buzzer technique.

This is a wonderful example of a modern, innovative approach that simply exaggerates the natural movement of the buzzers, and their attractiveness to vulnerable trout, to such an extent that it makes a huge difference to your chances of success. It should remind you just how much difference a new technique, or perhaps a new fly, can make and encourage you to be constantly experimenting to find this sort of advantage for yourself.

Fishing buzzers under a bung is so successful that some 'traditional' fly fishers refuse to use them. They limit themselves to straight-line buzzer fishing. Good luck to them!

There is little that is new under the sun. River fly fishers in the USA and New Zealand have been drifting nymphs along their streams under bungs for many years. It is very successful and some 'old fashioned' anglers there also resist it as 'too easy'.

As you are just 'getting started' perhaps it is better to taste success? Self-erected barriers can come later!

BUZZERS ON A 'WASHING LINE'

The first time you can actually see the rises of trout feeding on buzzer pupae is when they start to take them not far below the surface, at a depth of around 25 cm. These rises are not dramatic. The trout will be moving purposefully to mop up the ascending pupae but they do not need to chase them. Often all you see is a gentle bulge on the surface or, if they are slightly deeper, nothing more than a circular flattening of the rippled surface.

As the trout get even closer to the surface, these are replaced by exciting 'head-and-tail' rises. You see the fish's back leisurely cleave the surface as it moves from buzzer to buzzer hanging in the top 5 cm. It is difficult to stay calm as it looks as if a bonanza is on offer... but these trout can be hard to catch! Remember that trout hate to change their feeding depth, especially to go deeper, and your only chance is to present your buzzer imitations at the same depth as the naturals.

There are two options. The first is to use buoyant imitations. There are buzzer imitations tied with *Cul-de-Canard* feathers from a duck's preening gland to hold them in the surface. Other patterns incorporate a thorax cover of grey, closed *plastazote* foam. Both hold the flies close to the surface when fished on a floating line.

The second choice is simply to fish with a buoyant Booby lure as a tail fly with two buzzer imitations on droppers. The buzzers are suspended between the floating line and the buoyant Booby like clothes on a washing line as long as the whole set-up is pulled tight after casting. The heavier buzzer imitations will start to sink but a 'dead-slow-and-stop' retrieve will both keep them at the right depth and cause them to rise and fall attractively in the 'taking zone'. If the trout are feeding right on the surface and taking pupae suspended from the surface, it may be necessary to use two Boobies, one on the tail and one as top dropper, with buoyant buzzer imitations on two droppers between them.

When fishing close to the surface like this, there is one other essential trick. You must degrease the leader.

The reason for this is obvious. An insect like a buzzer pupae which is touching or breaking through the water surface will create a distinctive pattern in the surface film. This will not include a long line snaking away from it! If trout are swirling at a floating artificial but do not take it confidently, the chances are it is because a floating leader is putting them off.

THE 'EMERGING' BUZZER

The final chance a trout has to eat a buzzer that has ascended from the muddy bottom of a lake is at the moment when the pupa finally breaks through the surface film and 'emerges' as a flying insect. For Ephemerid flies such as Mayflies and olives this is a very vulnerable stage in their life-cycle as the emergence takes time and the adults struggle to adapt to an airborne existence and to take off. Classic chalk stream dry-fly fishing depends upon this fact and the trout's inclination to exploit it.

Buzzers are different. The pupa emerges quickly through the surface film like a submarine's periscope and transforms into a flying adult. It takes off instantly to join millions of others in their mating swarms in the lee of nearby trees. Their emergence on the water surface is the least vulnerable stage in their life-cycle and, at this stage, they are usually ignored by trout. Sub-surface pupae are much easier prey.

However, in certain conditions, the adult buzzer's emergence might not go exactly to plan and they get stuck in the surface film and do become vulnerable to trout predation. When this happens an artificial buzzer 'emerger' or 'crippled midge' pattern can then be a useful addition to the fly fisher's armoury.

Perhaps trout feed on emerging buzzers at times as their final option as a 'hatch' comes to an end and there are no pupae left to prey on below the surface, but it seems more likely that there are some weather conditions that do make it more difficult for the emerging buzzers to fly away successfully and that the trout take advantage of this. The emerging buzzers inevitably have problems during a strong wind, when, presumably, some are simply overwhelmed by the rough conditions. 'Emerger' imitations also work well on some days when there is a gentle, constant ripple and no gusting wind. These may just be conditions that make it easier for the trout to sip them down. They are certainly the conditions that the keen still water fly fisher who loves dry-fly fishing prays for.

As trout change from feeding on buzzer pupae that are just sub-surface to those emerging through the surface so does their rise-form. It changes quite dramatically from the leisurely 'head-and-tail' rise to an almost imperceptible 'sip'. It means you have to watch very carefully if you are not to miss it. So, do not cast far! If you find you have to fish at a distance, or if the ripple or light is awkward, the fly and arise to it can be difficult to see. Usually it is easier just to fish with a short leader and to watch the square metre or so of surface pointed to by the end of the floating fly line. If you see any tiny sip from any trout in this area, strike by lifting the rod firmly. It is almost certain this trout will have sipped down your fly. Some fly fishers improve their chances by using two or three dry or emerger flies on their leader on droppers. These droppers do not need to be far apart, 25 cm is enough, so that there is only a small area that you need to concentrate on to see 'sips'.

Remember that emerging buzzers do not move. The artificial buzzer emergers should be fished static.

It is always exciting to be able to cast to trout that are moving along the surface sipping down naturals. If one is moving in a straight line and remember to cast your flies 2 or 3 metres in front of it. However, if the sipping trout are working an area and their route is hard to forecast, as is often the case, it may be better just to cast into the centre of the feeding zone and to let them find your flies. It also means you have less chance of spooking them with repeated casts.

'Emerger' flies that imitate buzzers on the surface are not complicated. A body of red seal's fur is a favourite colour, perhaps because it imitates the flush of vivid red haemoglobin seen as the pupal skin splits to let the adult fly emerge. But, the absolutely essential property of 'emergers' is that they lie flat on the surface of the water or, even better, are half above and half below the surface film. They must not sit up on hackle tips.

One buzzer emerger imitation, the successful *Carrot Fly*, is nothing more than a tapered body of red seal's fur and six or seven turns of *cree* hackle, all of which is cut off below the body of the fly.

Another option is the *Klinkhammer* style of fly. These are tied on a curved hook with a parachute-style hackle so that the rear half of the body does penetrate the water surface. A floatant such as *Gink* keeps these flies 'in' the surface rather than above it. Klinkhammer patterns just need a dab of it around the thorax area of the fly.

Remember that the leader must be sunk for any dry fly to work.

AND FINALLY...

It is not surprising this section on buzzer fishing is the longest chapter on the tactics of fishing with imitative flies in this book. Still water trout feed more on buzzers than they do on any other natural food. They feed on buzzers at all stages in their life-cycle, but especially when their pupae rise to the surface to hatch.

The important message is that feeding on buzzer pupae often takes place close to the bottom. There is no indication of what is happening on the surface.

The second message is that the range of techniques that have been described to catch buzzer-feeding trout can all be adapted to catch trout feeding on other prey. Understanding, and mastering, the tactics needed to fool buzzer-feeding trout is a giant leap when getting started.

SUMMARY

HOW TO FISH WITH IMITATION BUZZERS
- Depth is critical.
- Dead slow and stop retrieve.
- Buzzer pupae move vertically not horizontally.
- Fishing buzzers under a bung is deadly!
- Use Boobies on the leader to keep buzzers at the critical depth.
- Keep the line and leader tight and the trout will hook themselves.

PART FOUR

NEXT STEPS

15
LANDING AND EATING YOUR TROUT

The final joy of landing a trout is to eat the fruits of your efforts. Good quality trout makes a wonderful meal.

There are two simple recipes in this chapter which are included only to help you with the basic skills of preparing trout for the table. You must be able to gut and to fillet a trout no matter how you are going to cook or smoke it.

Good cooking depends on the quality of the ingredients. It is a sin to catch a trout you are going to eat and not to make the effort to keep it fresh and in the best condition for cooking.

Of course, you do not have to kill trout and there is absolutely no point in doing so unless you or a friend is going to enjoy eating them. If you are going to release the trout you hook, you must do so carefully so that the fish swims away undamaged and survives.

PLAYING, LANDING AND RELEASING TROUT

If you are going to release the trout you hook, you must be well prepared to handle it with care.

DE-BARBED OR BARBLESS HOOKS

The hook on any fly you use must be de-barbed or barbless. Removing any barbed hook from a trout's mouth causes damage and extends the time taken to get it free.

You can buy barbless hooks but every shop-bought fly will be tied on a barbed hook. The barb is easily removed just by squeezing it with a pair of sharp-nosed pliers. Using hooks without barbs does not mean you lose more fish when playing them. It makes no difference at all whether hooks have barbs or not but, until anglers are convinced of this, hook manufacturers will continue to put barbs on nearly all their hooks and fly tiers will use them in order to sell their flies. The other advantage of de-barbed flies is that they are wonderfully easy to remove from your woolly jumper or, perish the thought, any other part of your anatomy!

PLAYING A TROUT

It is important that a trout is not fought to exhaustion especially if it is to be returned. Fewer fish are 'lost' if they are played 'firmly' to get them into the net as quickly as possible.

A newly hooked trout is often 'confused' and wallows near the surface when first hooked and it rarely reacts savagely. Competition anglers, for whom time is everything, sometimes take advantage of this to bully a hooked trout rapidly into their landing net before it realizes what is happening and regains its balance. However, once it does and panics, it will begin to fight in earnest. Some trout make long runs, others will jump again and again, some dive deep. Changing depth rapidly is their instinctive escape tactic. Trout that are hooked when deep in the water often rush to the surface as soon as they realize they are in trouble.

The basic advice when playing a fish is to *keep the rod tip up*. It can then bend further to cushion sudden runs and dives while still keeping plenty of pressure on the hooked fish. If your rod is not well bent you are being too gentle. Rods will always bend further!

If the fish really does set off for the horizon or the depths of the lake, you have to let it take line as it pulls the rod tip down. No matter how strong your arm you cannot resist the power of a strong trout to pull the rod down to the horizontal if you do not concede line. If you do not give line, the leader or tippet may break, the hook may straighten or, most likely, the hook will rip out! So, give line reluctantly and make your trout fight for every inch. As soon as it stops running or diving, retrieve line and put it under pressure again. Keep it under control. Get it to the net as quickly as you can.

All trout panic again, and will make a final run, when they are pulled into shallow water or towards a boat. Be prepared for this but be firm with the fish to stop it getting too far.

As the fight comes to a close, get the landing net into and under the water and *hold it still.* Do not chase the fish with the net! Lift its head and use the rod to slide it over the net, hopefully lying on its side. Wait until all the fish is over the net before lifting.

If this is the moment you realize you should have bought a bigger net, concentrate on getting the head in the net and then sweep it gently along the body. Where the head goes, the rest will follow.

How to play a trout is easy to describe. In the excitement of the moment it is equally easy to forget the best advice. You just need to hope you get plenty of practice.

USING THE REEL

Many new fly fishers worry about whether to play a fish using their reel, or by hand lining their fly line in using their free hand. Doing it this way means you have to pull the line over the index finger of your rod hand to control it.

Most trout are hooked after the retrieve has started when there are metres of line lying at your feet. If a hooked trout does not run all this line out on its first run, it is easier just to play the fish in by hand lining, using the index finger to clamp on the line if the fish is neither running nor 'willing' to be drawn in. The golden rule is to keep the line tight at all times during the fight. If it goes slack, all will probably be well but the hook may fall out.

If you have just hooked a trout, it is difficult to concentrate on keeping the line tight when you are also attempting to wind it onto your reel from the undergrowth beneath your feet! This is why most fly fishers hand line them in.

Of course, if the line is mostly on your reel when you hook the fish, you can play it directly by winding the short length of loose line onto the reel. Then you get the rare opportunity to use the reel's expensive drag system to control the trout's runs.

Beware! No matter how sophisticated the reel, you will still struggle to keep up with a trout that runs fast and directly towards you.

LANDING AND RELEASING IT

Any fish you are going to release must not be damaged by landing it.

Do not drag it up a rough bank. If you are wading, bring the trout alongside you in the water, run your fingers down your leader to get hold of the fly, and with a firm shake, remove it. The fish will swim off without being touched at all.

But, if you are standing on the bank or fishing from a platform or boat, you will need a landing net. It must be a knotless, soft nylon net so that it does not damage the fish's sensitive skin and protective slime. If possible, you should not lift the fish from the net at all. Run your fingers down the leader to the hook, grasp it and remove it. The trout can then simply be tipped back into the water without being touched.

If you must lift it out, perhaps to take a photo, make sure your hands are wet, grasp it firmly but not too tightly and get it back in the water as soon as possible.

There are un-hooking tools that cost only a few pence which are very useful, especially for removing flies that are well inside the trout's mouth. Occasionally, a hook will be right at the back of the throat and will be embedded in the fish's bleeding gills. This is fatal and the fish should be killed. No fish can survive damage in this area.

KILLING A TROUT

It is not easy to kill a trout for the first time.

You are holding in your hands a beautiful creature that has already given you the pleasure of its pursuit and capture. You can put it back to fight another day if you wish.

However, our desire to hunt and possess such wonderful fish was first driven by our need for food. You should not be ashamed to kill a trout to eat as long as this is from sustainable stock. This is not a problem if you are paying for a rainbow trout reared in a trout farm. If it is a wild brown trout, make sure your action is not jeopardising efforts to protect, conserve and increase the population of wild fish and the environment that supports them.

You need to be properly equipped to kill a trout. You need a small, weighted cosh known as a *priest* to 'deliver the last rites'. Any fishing tackle shop will sell you one.

When you have got a trout you are going to kill into a landing net there is no need to remove the hook from the fish or the fish from the net to delay the deed. Holding a fish still enclosed in the net makes it much easier to handle. Grasp it firmly round its middle with your left hand (if you are right-handed) so that your fingers are not too close to its head. Fish respond to touch so if you are tentative it will flap and you may drop it. Be bold! Do not try to hit it while you are holding it up in the air. Turn it upright and hold it against a solid surface such as the lake bank or a bench so that the top of its head is exposed. Give it a couple of hard hits with your priest on the top of its head right between its eyes. If you have hit it hard enough it will die instantly and will hardly twitch again. If it is still wriggling, hit it hard again.

It does take a little practice to do this quickly and effectively each time. Please respect your quarry. Get good at it!

KEEPING TROUT FRESH

It is a sin to let the freshest of food spoil through bad handling.

On commercial fishing boats their catch is gutted as soon as they get it onboard and before it is refrigerated. They know that fish rot from the inside outwards and that this process of decomposition is very rapid indeed.

To keep your trout at its freshest you should really gut it as soon as you have landed it and killed it. Not many people do this, perhaps because of the difficulty of disposing of the guts beside pristine fisheries and the need to clean up afterwards. However, many fisheries do provide gutting facilities in their lodges. If they do, you should use them as soon as you are able.

No matter how short the period between catching and gutting you should get into the habit of always squeezing the gut contents out of any trout through its vent as soon as you have killed it. Just squeeze your hand around and along its body from the head towards its tail. This will expel its lower gut contents and remove one source of the rotting process.

Any trout left exposed to the atmosphere, even when it is not sunny, will dry out and begin to decompose. If it is a warm sunny day this happens so rapidly a trout will be spoiled in an hour. A dead trout should be stored in a damp, porous bag kept in the shade. A bag specially designed for protecting newly caught trout is known as a *bass* and can be bought from any fishing tackle shop or website. A few years ago every bass was made of natural, woven straw but today synthetics dominate.

Under no circumstances store a trout in a polythene bag unless it is in a refrigerator. Polythene is not porous and even when the temperature is low a trout inside one will, quite literally, begin to cook.

Some anglers leave their trout in a bass submerged in the shallows while they fish on. This is fine if the water temperature is much colder then the air temperature, but if they are similar, as they usually are in summer, it is better to keep the bass damp by regular dipping and leaving it under the shade of a bush. The trout will be kept cooler by the water evaporating from the damp bass. If you can bear to carry a cool-bag and ice-cold blocks with you, so much the better.

GUTTING A TROUT

Preparing trout for the table is a skill all fishers need to master.

The first essential is a razor-sharp knife. 'Filleting' knives with long, narrow blades are sold in most fishing tackle shops and are a worthwhile investment. You also need to know how, and have the means, to keep them sharp.

The best surface on which to gut and fillet a fish is wood or plastic which is sandpaper rough and provides some grip. A normal kitchen worktop or smooth, shiny chopping board is positively dangerous. Newspaper does at a pinch.

Before you start you need to decide whether you are going to leave the head on a gutted fish or not. Many cooks like to serve up a whole fish at the dinner table so if you are freezing a few trout as gifts for friends or for future meals it may be best to leave the head and tail attached. They can always be removed later. However, if you do remove the head and tail it makes gutting easier.

First open the fish's belly by cutting through into the body cavity from between the gills and then along between the pelvic fins right along towards its vent. Do not cut into its vent which will puncture its intestine. Instead, continue to cut through the body wall to the side of the vent and just beyond it. Try to cut just through the body wall so that the tip of the knife's blade does as little damage as possible to any internal organs. It is especially important to avoid the liver and gall bladder which are not far behind the gills. The gall bladder will stain the flesh yellow if it is punctured. Be prepared for some resistance as you cut between the pelvic fins.

Do not worry if you do not get all this quite right first time!

If you are going to remove the head and tail, turn the fish on the cutting board so that from a start point just behind the head you can cut down at an angle so that you just go through the back bone. Then carefully cut round the body on each side of the fish so that your blade hardly goes into the body cavity until you reach the long, ventral cut you have already made along the belly. These cuts should go behind the pectoral fins on each side so that they remain with the severed head which should now be attached to the guts, but not to the body of the trout. Grasp the head firmly and pull it along below the body so that all the guts follow through the open belly. They will all come in one piece. Only the end of the large intestine will remain attached to the vent. You can either pull this to free it or neatly cut the vent out.

Now cut off the tail if you wish to remove it at this stage.

Finally, wash out the body cavity under a cold tap and you will see that all that remains is a wide line of 'blood' hard against the backbone which runs the length of the trout. This is actually its kidney. It would not do any harm to leave it there and would not spoil a cooked fish but most people remove it. All you need to do is to grasp the fish towards its tail with your left hand (if you are right-handed) and with your thumb inside its body cavity to give a firm hold. Then place your other thumb, facing towards its head end, at the rear of the kidney. Firmly scrape your thumb along the back bone to the head end of the decapitated fish to remove it. It is a messy business but plenty of running water helps.

If you want to retain the head and tail on a gutted trout the method is slightly different.

Cut open the belly of the trout as before from below the gills to beside the vent. Now, the tricky bit! Get your fingers round the guts to pull them out slightly so that you can get the point of your sharp knife into the body cavity up just behind its throat in order to make two forward cuts from each side to sever the gullet beside the gills. You can then pull all the guts out of the belly. They may not come out as cleanly as with the head attached and you might have to separately remove the transparent swim bladder and the heart from between the gills. You will also have to remove the kidney with your thumb as before. This is a little more difficult as the blood and tissue remain in the body cavity as you scrape it out along the backbone. Lots of running water will soon clear it away.

To do a perfect job you should also use a pair of very sharp scissors or some snips to cut out each pair of gills. Just cut through them top and bottom and remove them.

Trout freeze very well. The best way to pack them is inside 15 cm polythene tubing. This is available from most fishing tackle shops and websites. Pat the fish dry using kitchen paper, cut a suitable length of tubing and tie a knot in one end, put in the gutted trout, expel any air and tie a knot in the other end.

Job done!

COOKING THE CATCH

Trout vary in quality. The best rainbow trout for eating are those that have lived for some time in rich, fertile waters with plenty of natural food such as *Daphnia*. These fish will have lost the typical, internal fatty deposits and rather flabby muscles of newly stocked trout. Their flesh will be a firm, glistening orange and have exceptional texture and taste.

Recently stocked rainbow trout are fine but their flesh is pinker in colour and they are not as tasty.

Wild brown trout vary from firm, pink-fleshed fish from fertile waters where they too have a rich diet of crustaceans (although even the best examples do not display the fine texture and subtle taste of the finest rainbow trout!) to white-fleshed, rather muddy tasting fish from some upland areas. There is not much point in eating the worst examples!

COOKING THE TROUT WHOLE

In the UK it is rare to catch a rainbow trout which weighs under two kilos. Fear of cormorant predation means that fishery owners do not like to take the chance of stocking smaller fish. These fish are too big to be easily grilled or fried whole and should be baked in the oven or steamed in a fish kettle.

This is not a Jamie Oliver cookbook but here is an excellent recipe for baking a whole fish in the oven in aluminium foil. It does not matter whether it has its head and tail still in place for display purposes or not.

BAKED WHOLE TROUT

- Use a 50g knob of butter to dot the skin of the trout on both sides. Put any that remains in its body cavity.
- Place the fish on a large sheet of aluminium foil, turn up the edges, and season well with salt and ground black pepper.
- Cut a lemon in two and squeeze the juice over the trout; put the squeezed lemon into the body cavity with a few sprigs of fresh dill.
- Fold the edges of the foil together to form a neat parcel, put it on a baking tray and cook in a pre-heated oven at 200° Celsius (Gas Mark 6) for about 30 minutes or a little longer, depending on size, until cooked.

This trout can be served hot or cold. The cooked fish will be easy to skin and the flesh will separate easily from the bones. With practice you will be able to lift a whole fillet from the backbone.

FILLETING A TROUT

For many dishes you must fillet your trout. Trout fillets are also easy to divide into individual portions.

Filleting fish takes a little practice. Do not expect to get it absolutely right first time.

Again, the value of good lighting, a razor-sharp knife and a suitable, rough work surface cannot be over stated. If you are nervous of knife work you can buy protective chain mail gloves to protect your hands.

Start from the tail end of a gutted trout with the head and tail removed. If you are right-handed its tail should be pointing to your right and its belly should be facing you. Cut carefully, holding the knife blade horizontally, so that you begin to remove the tail end of the fillet from the backbone. Cut so that you can feel the knife just touching the backbone and so that the flat blade also cuts through the skin just above the mid-line of its back and belly so that it leaves the adipose, anal and dorsal fins on the fish. You can lift the fillet from the tail end with your finger and thumb to check your line is right but as you continue to cut you will also need to maintain some pressure on the fish with the heel of your left hand to keep it still. Keep other fingers high so that nothing is in the path of the blade. From about half way along the fish right up until the final cut you will feel the blade cutting through the ribs where they join the back bone. A sharp knife will cut through them easily.

When you have cut one fillet from the trout, turn it over and repeat the process to remove the other fillet from the other side of the fish. For some reason this always seems the more difficult side presumably because it is harder to get a good straight cut along the now more flexible backbone. It becomes easier with practice!

Discard the backbone and attached fins.

All that has to be done now is to clean up the fillets.

First, you have to remove the ribs. With practice you will be able to get the rib cage off in one piece. Place the fillet skin side down and hold it still with the free hand. The trick is to ease the sharp knife under the top of the ribs where they have been severed and then to run the blade, turned slightly upwards, below them. The whole rib cage joined by a film of connective tissue is all that should be removed.

Second, trim the edges of the fillet, including cutting off the pelvic films and their supporting skeleton.

The most awkward job is your last task. All trout and salmon species have a line of small 'pin' bones embedded in their flesh in a line along the fillet about half way between the line of the backbone and the top of the fish. If you find this line and run your finger along it you will feel the end of each exposed bone. They start at the head end of the fillet and peter out about half way along it.

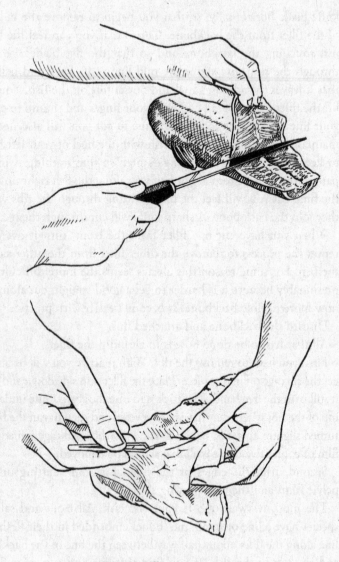

Fig. 39. Filleting a trout.
Top: Cutting the first fillet from the back bone.
Bottom: Removing the pin bones from the fillet.

They have to be removed individually. If you have strong fingernails you can pull each one out in turn, feeling for each new one with your fingertip as you go. They are much easier to remove using a pair of tweezers. You will find you tend to pull some flesh out with each pin bone but this is minimized if you pull in the right direction to separate them from their attached muscle. If you want to be really clever, you can run a sharp knife tip along the line of the bones to free them first. This task is a bit of a pain but some cooks prefer to do it this way.

COOKING TROUT FILLETS

There are thousands of ways to cook trout fillets. Enjoy them all! Here is the simplest recipe to start you off with some basic advice.

- The two fillets from a 1 kg/2 lb trout should each be cut in two to provide four portions. Pat them dry with paper kitchen towel before cooking.
- Heat some good quality olive oil in a heavy frying pan. Add the fillets skin-side down.
- Cook for 3 to 4 minutes depending on thickness. You will see the orange flesh changing to a light pink as it cooks. Do not wait for all of it to cook before turning it in the pan. When you turn the fillet press it down firmly into the oil. Do not cook this side for more than a minute or so. The aim is to ensure the fish is fully cooked but only just. It should be light and moist, not solid and dry!
- Serve with a thick wedge of lemon and a good dollop of tartare sauce.

Buttered, new potatoes, some fresh green beans from your own garden and a bottle of a New Zealand sauvignon are the perfect match.

Finally, do not forget that trout fillets are also great for hot and cold smoking. There are various fish smoking kits on the market. Most are excellent and give you the opportunity to experiment with wood types and an endless choice of marinades.

SUMMARY

- Use barbless hooks.
- Play hooked trout firmly.
- Avoid slack line when playing a fish by 'hand lining' instead of using the reel.
- Draw a played out trout over a stationary landing net. Do not chase it!
- If returning a trout, try not to touch it.
- Be bold when using a priest to kill a trout.
- Never store a newly-killed trout in a polythene bag.
- Gut a newly-killed trout as soon as possible.
- A razor-sharp knife is essential to gut or fillet a trout.
- Cooking a trout? Keep it simple!

PART FIVE

NEW HORIZONS

16

FLY FISHING IN RIVERS

This book suggests new fly fishers should start on a well-stocked still water rather than a river. Rivers do not demand more technical or casting skills. River fishing is simply more complicated.

It is easier to learn the basic skills of casting, fly presentation, hooking and landing trout before facing the complexity of a fast-running stream, tricky wading and a challenging range of trout habitats.

For some beginners, starting on a river may be their preferred or only option. This chapter helps. It is also aimed at 'improvers', eager to convert their new, still water skills to running water....an exciting step on the fly fisher's journey.

RIVERS AND ZONES

Every river across the British Isles is unique. The flow, fish and invertebrate populations of rivers change as they journey to the sea. For anglers, these differences and the 'fishy' habitats created provide endless pleasure and many challenges. Some anglers learn a little more about a favourite stretch on each visit; others prefer to sample the fishing offered in many different, beautiful river valleys. For all, the key to success is unravelling their quarry's relationship with its habitat.

There are two sorts of rivers in Britain.

RAIN-FED

Most rivers are rain-fed streams that gather water over mountain ranges and hills. As their tributaries come together, rivers grow. Their flow, still fed by ditches and other waterways, slows across coastal flat lands before reaching a tidal estuary. These rivers flood when it rains. In a drought, upstream sections are reduced to a trickle. Their trout are resilient fish!

CHALK STREAMS

In southern England, and in some lucky parts of Ireland and eastern England, there are 'chalk streams'. They rise from groundwater springs flowing from chalk and limestone bedrock. Although their volume falls if there are years of drought, or the groundwater is extracted, their flow is remarkably constant. They are crystal-clear and nutrient-rich. Mostly they flow steadily over downland and through fertile valleys to the sea. Chalk streams are perfect trout habitat!

ZONES

Fishery biologists divide most rivers into the 'trout' and 'coarse fish' zones.

There is no distinct boundary, but trout zones are upstream and mostly fast-flowing with a rocky or gravel bed where wild trout thrive. The only other large fish that is also found in this zone is the grayling *(Thymallus thymallus)*. Like trout, grayling is a *Salmonid* species found in cold and upland rivers across the northern hemisphere. Only fifty years ago, trout anglers treated grayling as unwanted 'vermin' in waters preserved for trout. Today, grayling enjoy equal status. Dedicated grayling anglers have formed *The Grayling Society*. Rivers such as the Frome in Dorset and the Teviot in southern Scotland are famous for big grayling.

Trout and grayling *mostly* feed on the stone flies *(Plecoptera sp.)* and mayflies/olives *(Ephemoptera sp.)* that are the dominant freshwater insects in this zone. The freshwater shrimp *(Gammarus sp.)* is an important part of their diet in chalk streams.

The coarse fish zone downstream where the river slows has more weed growth and often a softer riverbed. Here coarse fish, such as dace, chub and other species, dominate. Trout living here may have to migrate upstream to breed. There are more diverse invertebrate populations, and the water chemistry is likely to be enriched by agricultural run-off.

For example, the upland Welsh tributaries of the rain-fed Severn and the Wye, two of the longest English rivers, are trout zones. Most of the deeper, main river stems fed by these tributaries are in the coarse fish zone.

Further north, along the Pennine chain and in Scotland, the hills are steeper and the 'trout zones' are longer. There are plenty of coarse fish in the downstream sections of rivers in southern Scotland and its central belt. Pike and perch are usually the only coarse fish found north of the Tay valley. Trout dominate in the rivers and lochs of northern Scotland and the Islands.

A SHORT HISTORY OF TROUT AND BRITISH RIVERS
PRESSURE

Rivers and the fish that swim in them have been under pressure for a thousand years.

Before the Industrial Revolution they were dammed to produce the motive power for grain mills and to serve agriculture.

Scotland's native woodland, which would have covered the Highlands, had been cut down. Subsistence farmers were evicted to make way for sheep and deer, further denuding what had once been a temperate rain forest that acted as a huge sponge, releasing water and nutrients gently to rivers where trout would have thrived. Without the trees, rain rushes down bare hillsides. 'Spate' river floods take only a few hours to revert to dismal trickles when the downpour ends.

In the nineteenth century wild rivers were sacrificed to appease the gods of trade and commerce. Upland rivers were dammed to create reservoirs for public water supplies and to serve the factories.

Downstream, rivers became industrial and domestic sewers. By the end of the nineteenth century most northern England rivers that flowed through the new cities and industrial heartlands were biologically dead.

During the twentieth century there was no respite. A rush to harness hydro-electric power means that there is hardly a river system in Scotland that runs wild and free.

Bogs and marshlands across the British Isles were drained. Streams crossing arable land and new forestry plantations were straightened and dredged without any thought of the downstream flood risks. Healthy trout (and migratory fish) habitats and spawning sites were destroyed.

Historically, there was no statutory protection in Scotland for wild brown trout. Everyone had access, could fish by any method, and take any fish caught.

FLY FISHING CULTURE

In Victorian England, trout fishing was disappearing, and the unspoiled chalk streams of Hampshire were recognised as the *crème de la crème*. They became the preserve of the very wealthy. 'Fly fishing only' became *de rigeur*. A passion for identifying insect species and artificial flies that were exact imitations led to a cult of 'upstream dry fly only'. Anglers waited for a 'hatch' of emerging *'duns'* (see Chapter 14) to fish upstream for rising trout sipping them down.

This 'cult' was soon challenged. Trout continue to feed, and can often be seen, when no insects are emerging on the surface. They intercept nymphs and shrimps, which can be imitated by artificials, as they drift downstream. Debate raged. Eventually the rule became 'upstream dry fly or nymph only'.

Later, Frank Sawyer, a river keeper on the Wiltshire Avon, devised the Pheasant Tail Nymph (PTN), an artificial that used only pheasant tail fibres and fine copper wire, to secure its shape. This single fly, tied in size 14 hooks, served to imitate all Ephemerid nymphs. He also tied a grayling 'bug' that was shaped like a shrimp. He used the same copper wire and some darning wool he purloined from his wife. These were the only two flies he used. His book, describing these flies and how he used them, made him world famous. So much for 'exact imitation'!

Further north, rain-fed trout rivers upstream of the industrial devastation still held wild trout. Fishing rights were valued by local bosses and the professional classes. Many of the societies and syndicates they formed still manage these (usually 'fly only') trout fisheries today.

RECOVERY – GOOD NEWS

Debate continues, as it has since Victorian times, on the virtue of stocking rivers with trout. Today, those who believe that if you create a healthy habitat, then the ever-resilient wild brown trout will look after itself seem to be winning the argument. New management approaches on rivers right across the British Isles are bearing fruit.

'Catch-and-release' has become universal. The idea that wild trout are too valuable to be caught only once has boosted trout stocks in many rivers.

In Scotland, new legislation introduced Trout Protection Orders, and River Boards are now able to prevent unrestricted exploitation.

Active management is taking longer. But, while the jury is still out, it looks like the growing population of dam-building beavers in the Tay tributaries are working hard to create excellent juvenile trout (and migratory fish) habitat.

The best news of all is that many streams (but not all!) have recovered from a hundred years of industrial and agricultural pollution. A new cult of urban fly fishing for trout on rivers like the

Wandle in London and the Don in Sheffield is trending on YouTube.

Today is the first time for generations to be optimistic. Fly fishing for trout in rivers is on the up!

TACKLE AND EQUIPMENT

A 9-foot fly rod rated for a #6 weight line is fine for most river fishing. If you fish a hidden chalk stream surrounded by rushes and trees, casting a short line with a lighter outfit, say an 8-foot, #4 weight might be better. Recently, a new approach to nymph fishing, described below, has encouraged the use of longer (usually 11-foot) delicate rods rated for #3 or #4 weight lines.

Many river anglers never cast far. The dry fly fisher casting upstream to visible fish may never cast more than 8 or 9 metres. Assuming a 2- to 3-metre leader, this means only 6 metres or so of fly line beyond the rod tip. A fly rod 'works' when about 10 metres of the line (i.e. the head of a Weight Forward (WF) line is beyond the rod tip. This why beginners struggle with short casting when they use the 'correct' line weight. You must use a line that is rated much heavier, say #8 weight, with a #6 weight rod if you are only casting 2 or 3 rod lengths in front of you. Many river fishers also choose to use a Double Tapered (DT) line.

ACCESS TO RIVERS AND HELP

There is lots of trout fishing for all in rivers across the British Isles. Hundreds of clubs and fishing syndicates in the north of England, Wales and Ireland welcome new members, some provide day tickets for visitors. There are multi-access schemes in some areas of Wales and the South West that open many stretches to visitors.

In Scotland, major river beats on the Tay, Tweed and Spey are reserved for salmon fishing but there is good trout fishing available on their tributaries, and their upper reaches. There is no salmon fishing on Sunday and, if you enquire politely, it may be possible to sneak in for a day.

The major southern chalk streams are highly preserved and expensive. Some beats host costly corporate entertaining, others are fished by syndicates with restricted membership. The Salisbury District Angling Club does manage several chalk stream beats and sells a limited number of visitors' tickets.

Do not start your river fishing career on an expensive river Test beat. New golfers do not swing their first club on the Old Course in St. Andrews! Some commercial stillwater trout fisheries in the chalk stream valleys have sections of river you can try. This is a much wiser place to start.

Be choosy! All rivers are different. Trout numbers, their size, ease of access and fishing pressure vary enormously. Do your homework. Find what suits you.

Among the best are the Don and Upper Spey in Scotland, the Dee and the Usk in Wales, the Dove in the Peak District and the Suir in Co. Tipperary in Ireland.

Do not forget that rain fed rivers can be impossible to fly fish in flood and difficult when low. Perfect conditions are rare!

TUITION

Fly fishing in rivers is easier to demonstrate than describe.

Success is a perfect marriage of trout lore and river know-how. Food availability drives all trout whether they live in a steadily flowing chalk stream or a stream shaped by rainfall. Trout are territorial. They compete for a place that provides plentiful pickings. If you catch and remove a fish, its place in the current will soon be taken by another.

The expert's skill is knowing why and where trout lie, whether they are visible or not, and how to get a fly in front of them without them seeing you. This is usually more about 'watercraft' than casting technique.

This contrasts with stillwater fly fishing where long casting may be important, and you can often wait for the trout to come to you. In rivers, trout take up feeding stations in the current. Most fly fishers plan to move upstream or downstream seeking out likely lies or spotting fish. You will get an invaluable lesson if you make this journey with an experienced local guide who knows the trout lies on the stretch and has fished it in all conditions.

The value of fishing with a licensed guide (see www.game anglinginstructors.co.uk) cannot be overstated especially if you are a newcomer.

STEALTH

Occasionally, you will meet an unsuccessful river fisher who wears light clothes, stands tall, wades like an angry hippo and casts continually. Trout melt away in front of them.

Trout are nervous! They disappear when danger threatens. However, keep below the skyline, approach from downstream, wade quietly and slowly, cast only when in position and you will be amazed how close you can get to unsuspecting trout and grayling.

'Stealth', and the vital skill of wading carefully, is probably the river fisher's greatest asset!

RIVER TACTICS

WHEN

March to June is the best time to 'get started'.

On 'perfect' days on rain-fed rivers in March and April, much-loved anglers' flies, such as the March Brown, Large Dark Olive and the Grannom, hatch in big numbers. Every trout looks up to intercept the duns drifting downstream. The 'rise' can be short, and usually happens around mid-day.

Later, in May and June, mayflies emerge on chalk-streams. 'Duffer's fortnight' labels the peak of the mayfly hatch when the trout lose their normal caution.

By July and August most insect hatches end. Trout become moribund in high temperatures. These are the 'dog-days'. Your only chance is to fish late into the evening or very early in the morning. These are the months avid English trout fishers head north to holiday in highland Scotland.

In September, brown trout feed hard in preparation for spawning. Insect hatches are sparse. Terrestrial flies (most are black) blown on to the water and the year's crop of nymphs, hiding among the weeds and stones are plentiful. Fly fishing enjoys a final flurry.

Fishing for river trout is over by October. These days, many river fishers switch to grayling and fish for them throughout the winter.

WHERE?

All rivers are different. Trout are an adaptable fish and live in many different habitats driven by the availability of food and 'cover'. A preferred 'lie' is where the depth and current 'delivers' the most food. It is a perfect lie if it is close to deep water, weeds or an overhanging bank to escape from predators.

Chalk streams are mostly shallow with a steady flow unlike the steeper falls, turbulence, pool-after-pool character of many rain-fed rivers. On chalk streams weed beds, deeper holes, bends and footbridges create channels and plentiful lies for trout. Rain-fed streams offer more variety. Floods and droughts mean a good 'lie' today can be high and dry tomorrow. It is a tough place to be a trout.

On rivers that rise and fall dramatically, there are often shallow, fast-flowing stretches of undifferentiated gravel carved out and moved by each successive flood. These *'riffles'* have no stable stones or rocks to which nymphs and larvae cling. No trout live there either.

'Downstream a pool may be formed where the topography forces the river to bend and to dig out a deep hole. The 'riffle' becomes narrower, perhaps pushed against a high bank to create the fast-flowing, deep *'neck'* of the pool with much slower water alongside.

The *'crease'* between the two flows is attractive to trout. The fast flow concentrates any drifting food items. Trout lie in the slower flow, darting in and out to grab them. Any 'crease' between slow and fast currents is always attractive to trout.

Water entering a pool slows as the stream widens to form a *'run'* through it. Here the water is deeper, the permanent stones on its bed will shelter insect larvae and nymphs. This is prime trout territory, especially if one bank is tree-lined and roots provide protection.

At the *'tail'* of the pool it shallows, and the current accelerates before it cascades over a *'lip'* into the stream below. This is an ambush spot favoured by trout when nymphs are emerging.

Below many pools you will find a stretch with a permanent bed of boulders and rock. The depth changes where the current has cut channels through the obstructions. This is *'pocket'* water. In places there are perfect lies for trout where the current brings food, and the rocks provide easy escape from predators. It takes experience and skill to find fish, and to present your flies effectively here, but they are often the most satisfying trout to catch.

HOW - DRY FLY

Dry fly fishing is simple. You must ensure your artificial floats naturally into the sight of a feeding trout. Execution is the challenge!

Stone fly, olive or mayfly duns emerge from their nymphal skin on the surface of a river and are not able to fly away instantly. They simply drift inertly downstream for a metre or so until they can take off.

Any unnatural movement, or 'drag', of an artificial caused, say, by a tightening line kills the chance a trout will take it. 'Drag' is the major challenge for the dry fly fisher on a fast-flowing river. It is why you cast upstream and have to re-cast quickly as your fly drifts back towards you. Every cast risks scaring the trout. The expert gets into the perfect position unseen and gets the cast right first time!

Use a tapered nylon leader. It helps 'turn-over' to deliver the fly accurately. Keep leaders short. Shop-bought tapered leaders are 3-metres long. Cut it back to 2 metres, removing the thickest end, then add a metre of the lightest, degreased fluorocarbon tippet you can get away with. Fluorocarbon is heavy and sinks quickly. Trout are therefore not put off by a length of floating tippet snaking away from the dry fly.

On the smallest rivers, the leader should be even shorter.

Some fly fishers rely on a handful of dry flies. The ubiquitous 'F' Fly, tied on size 12 and 14 hooks in a couple of colours, is a favourite. It has a seal fur body with a wing formed from two or three highly buoyant CDC feathers from the preen gland of a duck. Users believe they are a passable imitation of any floating fly a trout sees. If they fish on chalk streams, they probably have a few mayfly imitations in their fly box too.

Other dry fly experts own a library of books that encourage them to carry hundreds of different dry flies that imitate the river's insects. They are a testament to their entomological knowledge.

Learn to cast a dry fly accurately over a vulnerable trout, and to cope with mischievous winds and capricious surface currents, before you decide which dry fly tribe to join.

UPSTREAM NYMPHING

On chalk streams where fish are often visible in the shallow water, a nymph-feeding trout is clearly active and alert. They are often described as 'on-the-fin'. You see them moving to intercept nymphs, usually within quite a narrow window and depth to save energy. Watch carefully and you will see a white flash as their mouth opens to grab their prey.

The challenge is to get your nymph, usually cast from downstream, into this 'killing zone'. Easy to say but casting a tiny fly so that it sinks to the 'right' depth without scaring the trout

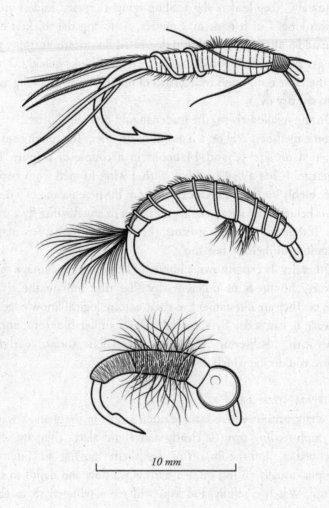

10 mm

Fig. 40. Three popular river flies.
Shrimp, Gold-headed Hare's Ear Nymph and Pheasant Tail Nymph

demands skill. Nymphs and shrimps are active swimmers. Artificials do not have to drift down as if they are dead. Experts practice moving their nymph as it enters the fish's sightline to 'induce' a take.

Many artificial nymphs imitate the 'real thing'. Even Sawyer's simple Pheasant tail Nymph (PTN) has a discernible tail, ribbed body, thorax and legs. Shrimp imitations (grayling love pink ones!) have realistic shell backs and soft hackle legs. Most nymphs are weighted with lead wire underbodies or gold beads to target trout (and grayling) that 'have their heads down' and would never rise to a wet fly or dry fly at the surface.

Fishing upstream or across in shallow water to a sighted fish is similar to casting a dry fly. Casting the nymph is more subtle. You have to calculate how long it takes to sink into the fish's eye line and decide if giving it a 'twitch' would induce a take. Again, easier to describe than to do. Years of practice help!

NYMPHS ON RAIN-FED RIVERS

On rain-fed rivers which are often coloured and turbulent – or in deep chalk-stream weir pools – it is usually impossible to see trout.

You must 'read' the water to figure where fish will be lying, guess their depth, get into position to cast, and aim for perfect 'presentation'. The nymph (or nymphs) on the end of your leader should trundle naturally along the bottom (they will get hung up at times) then lift attractively as the line tightens. You need to be stealthy. Getting unseen to a perfect spot to get the presentation just right, whether you are exploring a crease at the neck of a pool, a deep run below or pocket water among rocks, will demand silent wading or a hands-and-knees approach.

Fishing nymphs 'blind' presents other problems. Casting any distance, even a couple of rod lengths, makes control and presentation difficult. Fish can mouth, and then spit out, an artificial nymph instantly. You struggle to see, or feel, any take if you are metres away.

Recently, nymph fishing 'kit' has developed to address this challenge. Light eleven-foot rods rated for #3 or #4 weight lines provide extra reach and the ability to 'pitch' or 'lob' (it is certainly not fly casting!) heavy nymphs into the stream when 2 metres of line extends beyond the rod tip. This approach brings you very close to your quarry. It puts a high premium on stealth and careful wading.

When fishing 'blind' most nymph fishers use 2 or 3 artificials fished at 50-centimetre intervals at the end of short leader (under 3 metres) depending on the depth of the water. You put the heaviest, say a Gold-Headed Hare's Ear, nymph on the middle dropper. It dives to the bottom pulling the lighter nymphs with it. They flutter enticingly in the current further from the bottom. Beware of tangles.

FRENCH LEADERS

The most recent development is the *French Leader*. This replaces the need for a fly line for short range nymphing with a long rod. In practice, everyone attaches it to their fly line using a loop-to-loop knot. French Leaders are knotted, tapered (from 0.55 to 0.15mm) leaders, normally 12 to 16 feet long, designed to aid both the detection of takes and 'hook-ups.' Typically, the first sections use a high-stretch coloured nylon for extra 'give' when using a light tippet. Next is a short (15cm) 'high-viz' indicator followed by the final section of clear 4lb B.S. tippet.

With practice, this set-up makes it a bit easier to 'lob' and present heavy nymphs, and much easier to see takes by concentrating on the 'indicator'. You must strike firmly whenever you see the drifting leader stop, twitch or dart forward.

WET FLIES

On wider rivers, casting further across the stream and manipulating the artificial flies as they swing round in the currents, fast and slow, and among rocks and obstructions allows them to rise, fall back and drift just like the real thing. This technique, often described as 'downstream and across', is more subtle than that!

More than 100 years ago, 'Clyde Style' and traditional 'Northern Wets' to imitate the small, active nymphs of stone flies and olives were created by local fly fishers who fished similar upland rivers on both sides of the border. Unsurprisingly, the simple patterns have much in common, usually a waxed, silk body with a hackle from a common bird tied on a size 12 or 14 hook. Examples are the Partridge and Orange, Snipe and Purple and the Waterhen Bloa.

In a stream, the mobile, natural hackles hug the body of the fly into a nymph-like shape. Cast across or a little upstream, these flies sink a bit as they drift down until the line and leader tightens when they lift upwards just like a natural swimming up to the surface.

Wet flies are particularly effective in the spring when trout are looking 'up' for emerging nymphs. The trick is to 'work' the flies, especially in 'creases' between currents, towards the tail of pools and in 'pocket' water. The direction of cast, rod tip movements and the final 'hang' as the line tightens are critical.

LURES AND STREAMERS

Although they do not tend to publicise it, all river fly fishers know that not just dry flies and tiny nymphs catch fish. Trout are catholic feeders, and many succumb to a lure or streamer fly stripped quickly through the water. Most are a couple of inches long with a silver body to imitate a small fish, The place to try this tactic is in the bigger, deeper pools. It seems to work best when the water is coloured or high after rain or in failing light at dusk. Ten minutes lure fishing often provides a bonus at the end of a difficult day!

AND FINALLY.....

The wild brown trout and grayling that live in our rivers are wonderful, valuable fish. Please put them back!

SUMMARY

- Rain-fed rivers and chalk-streams demand different approaches.
- Grayling now enjoy equal status with trout.
- Trout populations, and many of the rivers they inhabit, are recovering from centuries of damaging pressures.
- Still water fly tackle is fine for river fishing.
- Use a licensed guide to help 'get started'.
- 'Stealth' is the river fisher's greatest asset.
- Learn how to 'read' a river.
- Subtle techniques and tactics need practice!

17

FLY FISHING HOLIDAYS

'Staycations' and 'activity holidays' are fashionable. There is nothing new under the sun. More than 150 years ago the Victorians 'discovered' Scotland. Whole families headed north each summer to stalk deer, shoot grouse and catch fish.

'Loch-style' fly fishing for trout from a drifting boat evolved. This perfect marriage of water, wind and waves is the best way to chase brown trout (and salmon and sea trout!) on wild waters in the Highlands and Islands and the west of Ireland.

This short chapter helps plan a fly-fishing holiday and have a go at 'loch-style'.

INTRODUCTION

Many hotels, estates and guest houses in Scotland and the west of Ireland offer trout fishing.

Absolute beginners are not welcome. Competent fly casting and an understanding of the basics are needed before tackling big waters. Fly fishing is no fun, even in glorious countryside, if you cannot cast.

Nobody tries to play golf without spending time on a driving range. Have casting lessons and practice before you go. Then, you'll master casting from a drifting boat surfing three-foot waves on a wind-swept loch.

Please take this advice!

LOCHS AND LOUGHS – BIG AND SMALL

Maps of the Scottish Highlands and Islands and the west of Ireland are peppered with lochs (loughs in Ireland) of all sizes. If you are staying in a hotel or estate, you will be told which to fish and those to avoid. A freelance traveller should consult Bruce Sandison's *Game Fishing in Scotland* or Peter O'Reilly's *Trout and Salmon Loughs of Ireland.* These 'anglers' bibles' are a little dated but are still a help.

HILL LOCHS

Across both countries (and in upland Wales and northern England) there are small, useful 'hill lochs' which are home to wild brown trout.

Some hill lochs are tough, acid environments where small trout struggle to find enough food. A few fertile lochs offer poor recruitment, but ample food, and trout grow big. Catching them may be challenging!

Starting on a loch full of tiny trout is fun. Action is guaranteed but even beginners get bored quickly. It is better to find one between 'easy' and 'challenging'.

Earlier guidance on small water fishing (usually for rainbow trout) applies equally well to hill lochs and brown trout.

Trout in hill lochs usually feed heavily on terrestrial insect blown onto the water. Use black flies to imitate them.

Brown trout tend to be territorial. Look for food-rich features that bigger fish may defend such as weed beds, burn mouths and shallows.

Keep moving! Wade carefully, if at all. Trout may not be far out.

SCOTLAND

Typically, in Scotland the less fertile waters are in long, deep glacial valleys or peat moorland.

'Productive' waters, which are usually shallower, occur where the underlying geology is calcium-rich. In Scotland, these are usually towards the eastern, coastal plain.

Loch Leven in Fife was once the most famous trout loch in the world. Unhappily, post-war agricultural 'improvements' to its breeding streams and serious industrial pollution have hit it hard. Although improving, it remains a shadow of its former glory.

Elsewhere in Scotland, there are patches of underlying bedrock responsible for some famous 'limestone' lochs in north-west Scotland and others in eastern Caithness. Productive trout lochs are also found in the Orkney and Shetland Isles. They are matched, or bettered, by strings of famous 'machair' lochs in the Western Isles. These shallow, coastal lochs, where trout prosper, sit over shell-grit and former seabed.

South Uist is home to some of the best. This island should be on every trout fisher's bucket list.

IRELAND

Ireland is a game fishing Mecca. Some peaty lakes are better known for salmon and sea trout, but the great limestone loughs of the far west are world famous wild brown trout fisheries. Loughs Corrib, Mask and Conn are the best known. These island-studded gems support a local economy built upon welcoming fly fishers and families.

THE BEST BIG WATER TROUT FISHERIES IN EUROPE

It will surprise many that the best big water trout lakes in Europe are within easy reach of London and Birmingham.

The reservoirs Grafham Water, Rutland Water (the biggest man-made lake in England) and Pitsford Water, are owned by Anglian Water to supply water across Eastern England. These 'pump storage' reservoirs source mineral-rich water from local rivers where control of agricultural run-off and other pollution has greatly improved water quality and clarity. There is no natural spawning but over 150,000 trout (mostly rainbows but some browns), weighing about two pounds, are stocked annually. The current fashion for catch-and-release means many survive to grow big. This rate of growth is phenomenal. A trout can double its weight in a year.

Some sneer these are not 'wild' trout but within weeks the rich feeding produces silver, torpedo-shaped fish of exceptional quality. They are selective feeders and a challenging quarry.

More trout from 4lbs up to double figures are caught each week from these reservoirs than are taken over a whole season from all the limestone lakes of Ireland.

Facilities for visiting anglers are good. Over fifty fishing boats are available every day on both Grafham and Rutland Water. Discounted three-day holiday permits allow you to choose where to fish. This is helpful. Sometimes one fishery is 'on-song' when another is 'hard-going'.

WHAT IS 'LOCH-STYLE' FLY FISHING?

A rowing boat drifts broadside in the wind. Two fly fishers, one in the bow and one in the stern, cast into 'new' water as the boat drifts down wind. They must retrieve and re-cast continually or it will drift over their lines and flies.

Traditionally, loch fishers cast a short line, around 12 metres, plus a 3- to 4-metre leader. Three flies, two on droppers, at metre intervals make up the business end. Perhaps a Black Pennel tail fly, lightly dressed on a heavy hook, then a winged Mallard and Claret, the top or 'bob' fly, might be a heavily-dressed Soldier Palmer.

Takes can come at any time but as the retrieve is completed, and the rod lifted to re-cast, the buoyant bob fly is drawn into to the surface film. Moving the rod tip sideways 'dibbles' the bob fly in the surface and 'hangs' the other flies. It's a critical moment. A following trout must grab a fly or lose it.

Watch for a swirl or the line tightening. Set the hook!

A library of famous books explores the magic of this simple but subtle technique. Repetitive casting needs stealth and precision. Rhythm develops. Concentration is vital. The wind can be challenging. Is it gusty or steady? How fast is the drift? Is it on a productive line? Is it over the right depth? Are fish rising? How fast

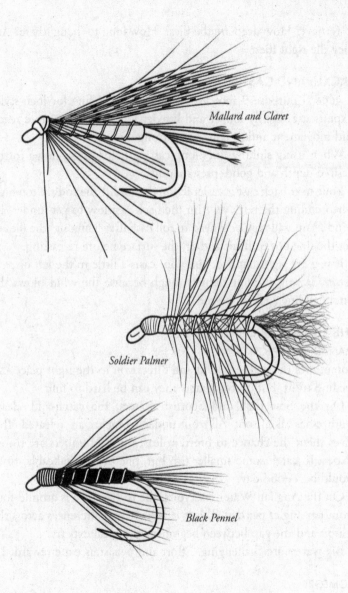

Fig. 41. Three traditional loch-style wet flies.

to retrieve? How deep are the flies? How long to 'hang' them? Are they the right flies?

TACKLE AND CASTING

A general-purpose 9 foot #6 weight fly rod is fine for loch-style. Experts use slightly longer and heavier kit to get a bit more reach and movement and to cope with strong winds.

When using sinking lines long casting helps to get down to the desired depth and good 'presentation'.

Your next back cast is easier if you do not lift the rod tip too high when ending the retrieve. Aim the back cast low to get 'under the wind'. You will regularly need to roll cast after 'hanging' the flies to get the line out in front and on the surface before re-casting.

If you are right-handed, aim your casts a little to the left or *vice-versa*. Casting to your right is tough because the wind blows the extended line against the rod.

THE BIG WATER CHALLENGE

MANAGING EXPECTATIONS

Sometimes the gods are kind and direct you to the right place and feeding trout, but on big waters they can be hard to find.

On the best Irish and Scottish waters, the catch-and-release culture has taken root. All trout under 13 inches are released. This gives them the chance to breed at least once. Numbers are rising. Expect to catch some smaller fish but, one or two 'takeable' trout would be a good day.

On the Anglian Water reservoirs, the rod average is around four trout per angler per day. This 'average' masks differences across the season and the gap between beginners and local experts.

Big waters are challenging. Effort and persistence are rewarded.

COMFORT

It is viciously uncomfortable to sit for a day in a rowing boat. The seat is hard and too low. The answer is a board and seat which lies across the thwarts of the boat and stretches your legs a little.

No matter the weather, you'll get wet. There is no shade. Waterproof trousers and sunscreen are essential.

Boats drift surprisingly quickly. All loch-style fishers use drogues (an adjustable, underwater 'parachute' which can be bought from any tackle dealer) to slow the boat and control the direction of drift.

COMPANIONSHIP, GUIDES AND GHILLIES

The essence of loch-style is two fly fishers happily sharing a boat and working as a team to agree (or not!) on location, tactics and technique.

For example, if buzzers are emerging, one can fish three heavy buzzer imitations deep while the other tries buzzer imitations or nymphs 'washing-line' style close to the surface. You'll soon learn what's best.

In Ireland, fishing with a boatman is usually compulsory. Most boat owners will not let you go afloat alone. *Take their advice!* Most loughs are dotted with dangerous shallows, winds are strong and unpredictable, and boats are valuable.

Your boatman will introduce you to the *'craic'*, a never-ending stream of amusing stories you'll not remember. You'll lunch on an island with tea from a Kelly Kettle. He'll know the lough like the back of his hand and do his best to find you a fish or two. It will be one of the best days of your life.

In Scotland, 'ghillies', usually more taciturn, do the same job. Using the oars, they'll keep the boat over shallows, a testing task on steep-sided lochs where short, on-shore drifts are essential.

On English reservoirs, 'guides' are available. Hire one for your first day. They'll demonstrate successful techniques and give you the confidence to go it alone.

CUTTING BIG WATERS DOWN TO SIZE

Big waters are overwhelming at first glance. There are thousands of acres to choose from. Where to go?

Experienced fishers' 'rule-of-thumb' is that 70 per cent of the trout are in 30 per cent of the loch or reservoir. They ask, 'Where were they caught yesterday'? If the wind and weather is similar, they will probably still be there.

Their usual approach to any day is to concentrate on a relatively small area. In their head the lake is divided into manageable chunks.

TROUT LOCATION IS DRIVEN BY FOOD

For example, in Grafham Water, trout gorge on emerging buzzers from March to May. Most of the pupae emerge from water between 3 and 7 metres deep, a 'buzzer band' between 50 to 100 metres offshore, around most of the reservoir. With eight miles of shoreline, it is still a large chunk, but usually one section, different each year, seems to be popular with both the buzzers and trout.

The loch-style fisher hopes for a wind blowing parallel to this favoured shore that allows long drifts along the 'band'.

ANCHORING

Many Irish and Scottish fly-fishing boats do not carry an anchor. After all, loch-style's purpose is to cover lots of water searching for well-spaced trout.

On English reservoirs, especially when buzzers are emerging, anchoring holds the boat over the buzzer-band and aids presentation of imitations, whether free-lined or under a 'bung', especially for trout feeding deep.

Anchoring causes disturbance. Give trout time to return but move on if you have no action after forty minutes.

In principle, there is no difference between fishing from an anchored boat and fishing from the bank other than having deep water under your feet.

Stabilise the boat with two connections to the anchor. Tie a loop in the anchor rope about 15 metres from its connection at the prow. Grab the rope halfway back to the prow and push it through the loop. This gives a doubled, adjustable length of rope which can be hooked over the rowlock.

WHEN

Trout are a cold-water fish and even Scottish lochs can be a bit warm and weedy by August, the traditional summer get-away.

Insect hatches peak in springtime. Buzzer emergence and hatches of olives take place from March to May in England and Ireland. The Scottish lochs are a bit later. The lochs of Orkney and the Hebrides are best in May and June.

The Irish mayfly hatch lasts form mid-May through June.

If you are stuck with July or August, head as far north as possible and climb the hill.

Many English reservoir fishers believe the best rainbow trout fishing of the year is between October and Christmas. Brown trout are out of season by then.

TACTICS

In principle, there is no difference in fly-fishing from a boat or the bank except when drifting you must retrieve line constantly to keep in touch.

SINKING LINES

You cannot wait for a sinking fly line to get to a chosen depth and good fly presentation is difficult, especially on windy days. Beginners must be able to handle visible, floating and intermediate lines before attempting loch-style with fast-sinking lines.

Most 'traditional' Scottish and Irish fly fishers never use sinking lines, simply because they always concentrate on relatively shallow water.

It is vital to mark sinking lines about 4 metres from the line tip so that you can see when to lift the rod tip to 'hang' the flies before re-casting. Use 'Tippex', covered with a length of the fine, shrink-tubing used by carp fishers, secured by a tiny drop of 'Araldite' epoxy at each end.

'TWIDDLING'

There is no perfect loch-style retrieve.

Inactive buzzer pupae, terrestrial flies and emerging nymphs are at the mercy of the waves. Often, the best retrieve is to 'twiddle' the flies back at the speed of the drifting boat. They are hardly moving, but you are 'in touch'. A heavy tail fly will sink a metre or so behind a floating line. The flies or lures will be dragged deeper by a sinking line.

WASHING LINE TACTICS

Using a sinking line and buoyant tail fly, such as a Black Booby, with nymphs on droppers and a fast initial retrieve creates an attractive wake before the Booby dives below the surface. Then, 'twiddling' back brings the nymphs into play.

Washing line and twiddling with a floating line keeps all flies close to the surface.

'PULLING'

On some days, trout ignore twiddled flies but are keen to chase fast-moving 'pulled' flies. Open-water *Daphnia* feeders often eagerly chase brightly coloured lures and traditional wet flies. Pulling at different speeds, using sinking lines that fish at different depths, can mark success or failure.

Cracking the code on the day is the charm of loch-style.

DRY FLY

Dry flies can be wonderfully effective fished in front of a drifting boat. They work best on cloudy, gentle days with a good ripple. Surface feeding trout are obvious, but often a dry fly will bring up trout to sip it down when there are no fish are to be seen.

You do not need many artificial dry flies. Use Black or Claret Hoppers on upland waters. On more fertile lakes a Big Red, Yellow

Owl or Midas are useful. Mayfly and Daddy-Long-Legs imitations are seasonal additions.

The body (usually seal's fur) of a stillwater dry fly must sit down in the surface film. Experts prefer flies with parachute hackles, or they cut away hackles below the body. Most use two or three dry flies on a short leader, thoroughly de-greased to ensure it sinks.

Cast frequently to cover the water in front of you. When you see a trout rise, it will be moving up-wind. Aim 3 metres in front of it. If you target the rise, you'll be behind it.

Dry fly fishing in a gusty breeze and big waves is testing. The individual flies are hard to see. Concentrate on the 3-metre strip beyond the end of your fly line; if a trout rises in this, strike firmly! The chances are it has taken one of your flies.

AND FINALLY . . .
Fly fishing is a journey. Plan wisely. Make every fishing holiday an exciting and rewarding destination.

SUMMARY

Going fly fishing usually starts a lifetime's journey. Helpful first steps are:

- Learn to cast and master the basics before you go on holiday!
- No two wild trout waters are the same. Work out why they are different.
- Scotland and Ireland are home to wonderful, wild places but the best 'big water' trout fisheries in Europe are in central England.
- 'Loch-style' fly fishing from a drifting boat is a perfect marriage of water, wind and waves. It's a team game. Learn with the help of ghillies and boatmen.

18

NEW HORIZONS

The novice fly fisher simply wants to catch a trout. The 'improver', who is enjoying new skills, wants to catch as many fish as possible. The tyro, perhaps now sated, simply wants to catch the most difficult fish. The unique joy of fly fishing is that, if you want them, there are always new horizons to find and new challenges to face. Some are exotic and expensive, but others may lie undiscovered on your doorstep.

The purpose of this book is to 'get started' on that journey without the false starts that delay and frustrate many. Fly fishing demands 'technical' expertise because you cannot start to fish until you can cast a fly but, from that point on, progress depends on understanding the behaviour of fish, their changing environment and their vulnerability.

In short, success depends upon the skills and instincts of the hunter, a human birthright that we all share.

WHAT HAPPENS NOW?

The advice in this book provides a particular insight on how to catch trout from small still waters simply because these are the waters where the vast majority of new fly fishers get started. It has been written from a UK perspective but, in practice, the basic advice applies wherever in the world trout swim.

Every new fly fisher will find it worthwhile to adopt a small still water trout fishery as their 'home' water. All such waters are unique. You need to study how the trout behave there, identify their food and the opportunities it presents to them and, therefore, their vulnerability. You are becoming a true angler when you realize that this learning process is as much fun as it is to actually catch a fish. And, inevitably, there will also come a moment when you suddenly realize that your home water is becoming predictable and perhaps too easy. Beware! It is a sign that fly fishing is becoming a passion that cannot be resisted. Broadening your horizons may change your life forever!

FISHING TACKLE AND FLY TYING

By this time you will also, no doubt, have become your fishing tackle dealer's best friend.

New fly rods, lines, reels and especially artificial flies will have become a source of endless fascination as you wonder if all the claims in their glossy advertising are true. You have to buy them to find out.

'Am I using the correct fly?' you ask, as a perfect cast in front of a cruising trout is treated with disdain. Then, another more successful fisher explains that he ties his own flies because, 'Those from the shop are not exactly what I want.' And, all the fishing magazines and books describe 'essential' flies that cannot be bought over the counter.

Finally, you realize that the cost of the hook and the slips of feather or tinsel that make up an artificial fly never add up to more than a penny or two and that a fly bought from the shop, which is likely to be lost soon thereafter, always costs at least a pound.

It is a no-brainer really. You need to get started at fly tying. The first new horizon has opened up. There are many more.

THE NEXT STAGES IN THE JOURNEY

The next progression in your fly fishing career is usually from small waters to big still waters.

This is, perhaps, the most daunting challenge. There is a world of difference between fishing a sheltered two acre lake and tackling the biggest, windswept lakes whether they are public water supply reservoirs such as Grafham or Rutland in the English Midlands, the large natural lochs of the Scottish highlands or the limestone lakes of the west of Ireland.

These big lakes are invariably fished from a boat to access their wide acres. Their trout are either wild or rapidly become so as they adapt to their multi-faceted new environments. The fly fisher has to adapt to lesser rewards in terms of numbers of fish caught and the physical challenges of a wild place. Casting skills learnt on a sheltered pond do not prepare you for a bouncing boat being driven across an inland sea by a gale force westerly wind.

You do not have to be limited to lakes.

River fishing opens the door to an entirely different environment. The trout may be of the same species but that is about as close as it gets. Rivers vary from lush southern chalk streams to gritty, northern rain fed torrents. Even the biggest of them always seem to be a more intimate environment than any still water fishery. Every pool needs individual attention.

You do not need to be limited to brown and rainbow trout.

The great lochs and lakes of Scotland and Ireland usually hold migratory fish. In some, salmon and sea trout are the principal quarry but, mostly, salmon and sea trout are caught from rivers. They are highly prized, wild fish and a deep pocket may be required to gain access to the best 'beats'. For many fly fishers it is a price worth paying.

You do not need to be limited to the UK.

The world's best wild trout fishing is probably to be found in Patagonia or the wilds of New Zealand. Trout were introduced to both areas by intrepid British explorers and immigrants in the nineteenth century. But, never forget that the best big lake fishing for rainbow trout in Europe is found in the English Midlands and is open to all for the modest price of a day ticket.

The world's best salmon fishing is on Russia's Kola Peninsula or in Iceland. It costs an arm and a leg. But, you can find salmon fly fishing on club waters in Scotland and Ireland for a few pounds; you just will not catch as many!

The best river sea trout fishing in the world is on Terra Del Fuego at the southern tip of South America. Good sea trout fishing can also be found in many rivers in Wales.

You do not need to be limited to fresh water.

Some of the world's most exciting fly fishing is for bonefish on the shallow coral flats of the world's most exotic holiday destinations such as the Seychelles and the Bahamas. You can also fly fish for mackerel, bass, mullet and pollock all around the coast of Great Britain, if you research where to find them, and it is absolutely free!

SUMMARY

Getting started at trout fishing on small still waters is usually the start of a lifetime's journey to explore the world of fly fishing. 'Destinations' to plan are –

- Learning to tie flies.
- Fly fishing from boats on big lakes.
- Tackling the challenge of rivers.
- Catching sea trout and salmon.
- Fly fishing in the sea.
- An endless choice of exotic species and places from the poles to the tropics.

Enjoy the adventure!

GLOSSARY

AMERICAN FISHING TACKLE MANUFACTURERS (AFTM) RATING

This is a worldwide standard by which the tensile strength of fly rods and the weight of the fly lines they cast are determined. It means that no matter where in the world you buy a fly rod or a fly line a #7 weight rated rod is designed to cast a #7 weight rated fly line. Rods and lines vary from an ultra-light weight #1 weight to #14 weights designed to cast heavy flies at, and to land, oceanic giants such as marlin.

ARTIFICIALS

Generic name for all artificial flies.

ATTRACTOR FLY

A fancy fly pattern simply designed to attract rather than to specifically imitate a prey species. See **lure** below.

BASS

A proprietary bag or sack designed to keep newly caught fish fresh. There are many types on the market.

BLOB

Lures tied with a thick body of fluorescent *Fritz* chenille. There are many colours and variations. They do not have tails. Originally tied without tails to be compliant with competition rules on fly length.

BOOBY

A buoyant fly created by incorporating two balls of buoyant *plastazote* foam into its dressing at the head of the fly.

BUGS

Small, highly weighted lures used for catching visible fish in clear water fisheries, sometimes in quite deep water.

BUZZERS

This is the anglers' name for the commonest insects found in lakes and rivers. The generic name is *Chironomus sp*. Their common name is 'non-biting midges'. Their life-cycle is *egg>larva> pupa>flying adult*. Fly fishers and trout are most interested in the pupae. They are heavily predated upon as they float up to the surface to emerge as flying adults. A high pitched 'buzz' is heard as they fly by, thus their name.

CARROT FLY

A dry fly tied with a tapered, red seal's fur body and a cree hackle. Usually used to imitate adult buzzers.

CREE HACKLE
A black and white barred hackle feather used to tie many dry flies.

DAMSELFLY LARVAE
20 mm insect larvae (nymphs) found in all still waters. They hatch into the familiar bright blue damselflies from late June until September. They normally crawl up plant stems to emerge as adults but many swim actively to the surface and are vulnerable to trout predation.

DAPHNIA
Pin-head-sized 'water fleas' that *bloom* (i.e. their population explodes) at any time between April and October. Only found in fertile waters.

DRY FLIES
Flies designed to float on the surface of the water. They normally imitate and are named after an individual insect species such as Daddy-Long-Legs. They are usually *tied* using stiff, neck hackles from specially bred cockerels that ride on the surface film.

DUBBED
The use of a waxed thread onto which fur is twisted to form the body of an artificial fly.

EMERGERS
Are flies designed to sit 'in' the surface film and to imitate the vulnerable stage in the aquatic insect life-cycle when an immature nymph or pupa pushes through the surface-film and splits open to emerge as an adult

flying insect. They are *tied* with a small amount of buoyant material to support the body of the fly which sinks below the surface film.

FLY
Any hook *dressed* with feathers, fur or synthetic materials no matter whether it imitates an insect or not is known as a fly as long as it is light enough to be cast by a fly rod and fly line. It must not incorporate any edible bait.

FLY LINE
A thick, plastic-coated line which is usually tapered and which provides the weight to cast an almost weightless fly on a short, fine leader. Fly lines are designed to sink or to float. Sinking lines are made and graded to sink at different speeds. Different manufacturers have a range of specifications for their sinking lines.

FLY 'PATTERN'
The recipe of materials that make a specific fly is the 'pattern'. Some fly patterns have been recorded for over 100 years.

FLY REEL
A reel designed with a spool to accommodate a fly line and to be used on a fly rod.

FLY ROD
A flexible rod designed to cast a heavy fly line and an almost weightless artificial fly.

GINK
A proprietary, silicon gel used to help dry flies to float. There are various similar products available.

GOLD HEAD
A fly pattern which incorporates a gold bead.

HATCH
The period when freshwater insects are emerging from the water or otherwise become vulnerable to trout predation.

HOPPERS
Dry, i.e. floating, flies tied with knotted pheasant tail fibre 'legs' to imitate a natural insect.

KLINKHAMMER HOOKS
Bent hooks designed to create emerger flies that are fished 'in' rather than 'on' the surface film.

LAKE AND POND OLIVES
'Up-wing' *Ephemerid sp.* flies in the same family as Mayflies which hatch out on the surface during April and May on many still waters. They are about 10 mm long. Their dark brown nymphs are active swimmers which swim to the surface to hatch in large numbers from the shelter of the lake bed. Trout respond accordingly. In upland lakes similar up-wing species hatch throughout the summer. Their nymphs and adults probably make up the bulk of trout food in these lakes alongside terrestrial insects that are blown onto the water.

LANDING NET
A net with a handle used to lift a hooked fish from the water.

LEADER
The length of fine nylon monofilament or fluorocarbon line tied onto the fly line to which a tippet and fly are tied. Beginners are advised to use tapered leaders to aid casting.

LINE TRAY
A net or other tray into which the fly line falls tidily to prevent tangles during casting.

LURE
Any fly that does not imitate an obvious prey species but is still attractive to trout. Often incorporates brightly coloured material. **Lure** is also used to describe a fly that is designed to imitate a small fish.

MAYFLIES
Ephemera danica is the best known of the insects that hatch each year on the chalk streams of southern England. Mayflies also inhabit fertile ponds and lakes, especially in the valleys of the chalk streams, but isolated populations are found throughout the UK and Ireland. Their larvae are vulnerable to trout predation when they leave their permanent home in muddy margins to hatch from May until August. The flying adults are eaten at both stages in their short adult life-cycle.

PRIEST
A short cosh-like tool used to kill fish. There are many designs on the market.

PULL
Another word for a **take**.
RED GAME and CREE
Popular colours of hackle feathers used to tie flies.

RETRIEVING
Using the free hand to pull the fly line through the rod rings after casting so that the fly on the end of the leader moves through the water back towards the fisher. The retrieved line is allowed to fall on the ground at his or her feet.

RISE
This word has two meanings. It is an individual trout visibly breaking the water surface perhaps to eat a floating insect. Or, it is an 'event' when a lot of insects are emerging from the water or being blown onto it and many trout are visibly responding to this feeding opportunity to create a *feeding frenzy*. Trout are usually seen **rising**.

RISE, TAKE or PULL
When a trout engulfs an artificial fly and this is either seen or felt by the angler.

SHRIMPS
Gammarus sp. are found in fertile still waters although they are more at home in streams. They favour gravel bottoms and weed beds, and trout tend to find them along with other prey like damselfly nymphs when they are prospecting for food rather than selectively feeding on one species.

SMALL FISH OR FRY
All trout eat little fish if they are available. In lowland waters this usually means coarse fish which can form huge concentrations of tiny 5 mm-long newly hatched fry in June. They become 'available' again when the weed cover dies back in the autumn. By this time they are 40 mm long. In upland waters where there are fewer prey fish they are rarely found in trout stomachs.

SNAILS
Occasionally, usually in mid-summer, trout can gorge on water snails. Snails spend most of their time on the weeds they eat. Sometimes a wind dislodges them from a weed bed and air in their shells prevents them from sinking. They then drift across open water suspended from the surface film and trout are attracted to this bounty. At other times some trout seem to develop so much of a taste for snails that their stomachs almost rattle when caught. There is no need to spoon them!

STOCKIES
Newly stocked rainbow trout.

TAKE
The pull on the line felt when a trout takes your fly.

TERRESTRIAL FLIES
On upland waters a wide variety of terrestrial flies, grasshoppers and beetles that are blown accidentally onto the water's surface are probably

what their trout eat most during the summer. In lowland agricultural areas there are generally fewer flying insects but there are sometimes large, local eruptions in numbers that can create a 'windfall' for trout in nearby still waters. The best known examples are black Hawthorn Flies in May and Daddy-Long-Legs in September. Neither hatch is guaranteed to happen but it is wise to be prepared.

TIPPET
A short length of fine line to which the fly is attached, usually on the end of a tapered, nylon monofilament leader.

VARYING THE RETRIEVE
The purpose of retrieving the fly is to make it move so that it is attractive to trout, perhaps imitating an actual insect. Changing the speed of the retrieve, or stopping and starting, may be better than a uniform speed.

WATER BOATMEN
Corixa sp. are beetles that are common in all waters. They are recognized by their large paddle-like front legs and jerky swimming style. They float up to the surface from time-to-time to replenish air they carry with them which often looks like a silver bubble and is highly visible. Their numbers increase during the summer and they become vulnerable when the weeds die back in autumn. This is when they are most likely to be eaten by trout.

WATER HOG LICE
Asellus sp. are woodlice-like crustaceans that are common in fertile still waters. They prefer a stony lake bed or one with plenty of weed or detritus cover where they can hide from trout and other predators.

WEIGHT FORWARD FLY LINE
Fly lines are made with different tapers and profiles. A weight forward line has its weight concentrated into its first 10 metres or so. This tapered *head* is followed by a much finer *running line* to help the line *shoot* a long way when it is cast.

WEIGHTED FLY
A fly which incorporates extra weight (usually lead wire) to make it sink more quickly.

WET FLIES
Are flies that are designed to be fished below the surface of the water. They are traditionally *tied* using natural fur and softer neck feathers (*hackles*) that sink easily through the surface film. They imitate insects during the sub-surface stage of their life-cycle. Some wet flies are tied using much more colourful materials and colours. The most garish and largest are known as lures. Another group of 'wet fly' are those known as 'nymphs'. These are specifically tied to imitate the sub-surface stage of aquatic insects. Flies are often named after their originator, e.g. *Wickham's Fancy* or from the materials used, e.g. *Gold-Ribbed Hare's Ear Nymph (GRHE)* or their colour, e.g. *Orange Blob*. Some are named after the insects they imitate e.g. *Buzzer*.

APPENDIX – SELECTED TROUT FISHERIES

ENGLAND AND WALES
Most of the following fisheries are members of the Stillwater Trout Fisheries' Association (www.troutfisheries.co.uk). Other fisheries can be found on their website.

CENTRAL ENGLAND
• Elinor Trout Fishery, Nr. Kettering, Northamptonshire.
www.elinortf.co.uk

• Fisherwick Lakes, Nr. Lichfield, Staffordshire.
www.fisheries.co.uk/fisherwick

• Lechlade Trout Fishery, Lechlade, Gloucestershire.
www.lechladetrout.co.uk

• Lenches Lakes, Nr. Evesham, Worcestershire.
www.lencheslakes.co.uk

• Patshull Park Fishery, Pattingham, Shropshire.
www.patshull-park.co.uk

• Ravensthorpe Reservoir, Ravensthorpe, Northamptonshire.
www.anglianwater.co.uk/leisure

• Roxholme Grange Fly Fishing, Carlton-in-Lindrick, Nottinghamshire.
www.roxholmetrout.com

• Salford Trout Lakes, Nr. Chipping Norton, Oxfordshire.
www.salfordtroutlakes.co.uk

• Thornton Reservoir, Thornton, Leicestershire.
www.flyfishthornton.co.uk

• Toft Newton Trout Fishery, Nr. Market Rasen, Lincolnshire.
www.toftnewton.com

EASTERN ENGLAND
• Chigboro' Fisheries, Nr. Maldon, Essex.
www.chigborofisheries.co.uk

• Rib Valley Fishing Lakes, Nr. Ware, Hertfordshire.
www.ribvalleyfishinglakes.co.uk

SOUTH EAST ENGLAND
• Albury Estate Fishery, Nr. Albury, Surrey.
www.alburyestate.com

• Hayes Street Farm, Nr. Bromley, Kent.
www.hayesstfarm.co.uk/flyfishing-trout-lake-bromley.html

• Syon Park Fishery, Nr. Brentford, Middlesex.
www.alburyestate.com

• Tenterden Trout Waters, Tenterden, Kent.
www.tenterden-trout-waters.co.uk

SOUTH WEST ENGLAND
• Exe Valley Fishery, Nr. Dulverton, Somerset.

• Fernworthy Reservoir, Nr, Chagford, Devon.
www.swlakestrust.org.uk/leisure-activities

• Flowers Farm Trout Lakes, Nr. Dorchester, Dorset.
www.flowersfarmlakes.co.uk

• Kennick Reservoir, Bovey Tracey, Devon.
www.swlakestrust.org.uk

• Wistlandpound Reservoir, South Moulton, Devon.
www.swlakestrust.org.uk

• Witcombe Waters, Great Witcombe, Gloucestershire.

SOUTHERN ENGLAND
• Barn Elms Fly Fishery, Nr. Reading, Berkshire.
www.barnelmsfishery.co.uk

• Church Hill Fishery, Mursley, Buckinghamshire.
www.church-hill-fishery.co.uk

• Haywards Farm Fishery, Theale, Berkshire.
www.haywardsfarmfishery.co.uk

• Meon Springs Fly Fishery, Nr. Petersfield, Hampshire.
www.meonsprings.com

NORTH EAST ENGLAND
• Fontburn Fishery, Nr. Morpeth, Northumberland.
www.nwl.co.uk/your-home/leisure/fontburn-reservoir.aspx

• Sharpley Springs, Seaham, Co. Durham.
www.sharpleysprings.blogspot.co.uk

NORTH WEST ENGLAND
• Bank House Fishery, Caton, Lancashire.
www.bankhouseflyfishery.co.uk/

• Danebridge Fisheries, Wincle, Cheshire.
www.danebridgefisheries.com

SCOTLAND
These Scottish small trout fisheries are all featured in www.fishpal.com/scotland. Many other Scottish trout fisheries are detailed there.

EAST CENTRAL SCOTLAND
• Markle Fishery, East Linton, East Lothian.
www.marklefisheries.com

NORTH EAST SCOTLAND
• Forbes of Kingennie Country Resort, Nr. Dundee.
www.forbesofkingennie.com

NORTH SCOTLAND
• Mossat Fishery, Alford, Aberdeen-shire.
www.mossattroutfishery.co.uk

SOUTH EAST SCOTLAND
• Coldingham Loch, Eyemouth, Berwick-shire.
www.coldinghamloch.co.uk

SOUTH WEST SCOTLAND
• The Green Frog, Hammerlands, Moffat, Dumfries-shire.
www.moffatfishery.co.uk

WEST CENTRAL SCOTLAND
• Carbeth Fishery, Blanefield, Stirling-shire.
www.sites.google.com/site/carbethfishery

WEST COAST SCOTLAND
• Inverawe Fishery, Taynuilt, Argyll-shire.
www.inverawe-fisheries.co.uk

NORTHERN IRELAND
Details of all small trout fisheries in Northern Ireland can be found at www.nidirect.gov.uk/index/angling

CO. ANTRIM
• Middle South Woodburn, Nr. Carrickfergus.

CO. DOWN
• Loughbrickland Lake, Banbridge.

HELPFUL SHOPS, WEBSITES AND MAGAZINES

FISHING TACKLE SHOPS

ANGLIAN WATER
• Rutland Water Fishing Lodge,
Edith Weston, Oakham,
Rutland, LE15 8HD

• Grafham Water Fishing Lodge,
Perry,
Nr. Grafham,
Cambridgeshire, PE28 0BX

• Pitsford Water Fishing Lodge,
Brixworth Road,
Holcot,
Northamptonshire NN6 9SJ

• Anglian Water's fly fishing mail
order phone number is 01780 686441

BELFAST ANGLING CENTRE
• Argyle Business Centre,
North Howard Street,
Belfast, BT13 2AU
Tel. 028 9031 3156
www.fishingtackle2u.co.uk

FARLOWS
• 9, Pall Mall,
London SW1Y 5NP
Tel. 020 748 410000
www.farlows.co.uk
www.sportfish.co.uk

GLASGOW ANGLING CENTRE
• Unit 1, The Point Retail Park,
29, Saracen Street,
Glasgow, G22 5HT
Tel. 0871 716 1670
www.fishingmegastore.com

JOHN NORRIS OF PENRITH
• 21, Victoria Road,
Penrith,
Cumbria, CA11 8HP
Tel. 01768 864211
www.johnnorris.co.uk

SPORTFISH
• Winforton,
Hereford, HR3 6SP
Tel. 01544 327111
www.sportfish.co.uk

HAYWARDS FARM
• Theale, Reading, RG7 4AS
Tel. 01189 303860
www.sportfish.co.uk

FISHING TACKLE MAKERS' AND SUPPLIERS' WEBSITES
• www.airflofishing.com
• www.greysfishing.com
• www.orvis.co.uk
• www.snowbee.co.uk
• www.tightlines.co.uk

LEAD BODY FOR ANGLING
(INCORPORATING THE ANGLING DEVELOPMENT BOARD)
• Angling Trust and Fish Legal,
Eastwood House,
6, Rainbow Street,
Leominster,
Herefordshire, HR6 8DQ.
Tel. 0844 7700616
www.anglingtrust.net

INSTRUCTION FROM LICENSED COACHES FROM THE GAME ANGLING INSTRUCTORS' ASSOCIATION
• www.gameanglinginstructors.co.uk

MAGAZINES
• *Trout & Salmon* published by Bauer
Consumer Media Ltd.
www.greatmagazines.co.uk

• *Fly Fishing & Fly Tying* published by
Rolling River Publications Ltd
www.flyfishing-and-flytying.co.uk

All are published monthly.

INDEX